Dave,

BETTER THAN
YOU THINK

To the
Good Life!

BETTER THAN YOU THINK

Developing Awareness for a More Fulfilling Life

ROBERT COMMODARI

STOREHOUSE
MEDIA GROUP

LCCN: 2019917244

Paperback ISBN: 978-1-63337-337-2
E-book ISBN: 978-1-63337-668-7

Printed in the United States of America

1 3 5 7 9 10 8 6 4 2

CONTENTS

To those desiring a fulfilling life through increased awareness.

&

To my parents and beautiful family.

INTRODUCTION

HOW IS IT POSSIBLE that we live life at ninety miles an hour but never seem to get to where we want to be? Why do we have more material goods, more access to information, more ways to interact than ever before, yet still feel unfulfilled? Why are we better off than any society in history yet often feel tapped out, unmotivated, overworked, and unsatisfied?

Each of those questions has the same answer: We are not practicing awareness.

That statement seems pretty simple on the surface, but to practice awareness, you have to stop: stop running from one activity to the next; stop comparing yourself to everyone else; stop trying to be who others think you should be. When you stop all of these things, you give yourself space to quiet your mind, reflect on your experiences, and get to know yourself better. And when you know yourself better, you can identify what you want out of life and pursue it, which leads to a more fulfilled life.

The journey to fulfillment begins with an awareness of who

you are. Traveling a road of personal growth, you will become aware of what makes you tick—what gives you energy when you think about a certain topic, subject, or pursuit—and what drains every last drop of energy. You may not always like what you discover, but you will be inspired by it. The point is to become aware of who you are and who you're becoming. The journey of self-awareness is powerful because increased awareness brings increased understanding, and increased understanding empowers you to make changes in your life that last.

As you observe and contemplate what you see happening within you and around you each day, you will gain a new and freeing perspective: You may find yourself letting go of unhealthy attachments to people, places, acknowledgement, ideas, and many other things. These attachments prevent us from living the life we were designed to live, from being the best we can be, because they subtly (and sometimes, not so subtly) steer us to live according to someone else's standards instead of our own. When we do this, we often become unhappy, experiencing that feeling of "something missing" because we aren't being true to ourselves. Some people mistakenly believe the solution is to try to completely change their lives, and the effort overwhelms them and ultimately depresses them further. But if you do the work I suggest in this book, you will discover through your new awareness practice that your life doesn't need a complete overhaul, because your life is already better than you think. *You* are already better than you think. And that realization will become the "special sauce" that fuels everything else you tackle on your journey to a more fulfilling life.

I've written this book to inspire you to reflect on your life experiences and become aware of all the good that has occurred and is occurring in your life. I've also written it to help you learn to better deal with the not-so-good moments that are inevitable, so that everything you experience moves you forward instead of setting you back. I will share my experiences and the lessons I have learned in my life in hopes that they will help you discover lessons from the experiences *you* have had. Becoming aware of these lessons and applying them will help move you forward toward a life filled with peace, happiness, and joy.

But understand this: Once we have a moment of fulfillment, the journey doesn't stop. We're not always going to stay there in the land of peace, happiness, and joy. A moment of fulfillment may last only an instant. For example, you may have been teaching your child to understand a concept for years and out of nowhere your child may say something that connects back to what you were teaching. In that moment you say to yourself, "They finally get it." And you feel fulfilled as a parent, until the next moment, when they cause trouble in some new way.

However long the feeling of fulfillment lasts, it's never permanent. Things happen, we get distracted, life throws us curveballs, and we lose that sense of fulfillment for a period of time.

Your life may be better than you think, but sometimes it really doesn't feel that could be true.

So, in those moments, how do we find fulfillment again? It's a journey, and when we reflect back on our days, our weeks, or even our lives, we can see where we may have found fulfillment and when we may have been unsure of where to find it. Practicing awareness is a way to ensure you find your way back sooner and with less effort, and less pain along the way. It's a habit that shifts the balance in your life to feeling fulfilled more often than not.

This book is about my journey and the lessons I have learned that have allowed me to experience more fulfilling moments. You will experience my struggles and successes and read about my perspective on these experiences. You will understand how by becoming more aware, I was able to understand those experiences as lessons. I was able to come to a place where I realized my life was better than I thought. And I learned, as you will, how to spend more time benefitting from that perspective.

Although our stories are different, there may be something in my stories that resonates with you and helps you reflect on your life. Maybe you never thought of something you experienced as an opportunity to learn. Maybe something happened to you, and until you connected it with my story, it didn't resonate with you. But after thinking about my experience, you have an "ah-ha" moment regarding your own experience and an understanding of why things happened the way they did. This is awareness. Enough awareness leads to the realization that your negative thoughts, fears, and hang-ups—and those put upon you by others—are simply hiding the things about your existence that are already wonderful. You begin to see more clearly.

When you can more clearly examine your own feelings in the context of the history of your life and environment, you gain understanding of how you became you. And as you reflect on your experiences, whether those that happened this morning or those that happened a decade ago, you become more practiced at awareness, and it becomes a habit. That habit leads to more fulfilling moments. Enough fulfilling moments lead to a general feeling of fulfillment.

At least, until life throws another curveball.

But again, that's why I've offered up this guide. Think of it as a roadmap and a source of inspiration you can turn to again and again. When you're ready to read a chapter or two, set aside a small chunk of time and find a quiet place with no distractions. As you read through each chapter, you may want to pause to reflect on what you have read before moving to the next chapter. I have included questions in each chapter to help you reflect on the experiences and stories of your life. You may also keep a journal nearby to write down your reflections and the lessons you have learned from your experiences. This is how you build (and maintain) a habit of awareness. (To help you, grab the free companion workbook at robcommodariauthor.com/workbook.)

Fulfillment starts within, by becoming aware of all that is happening and understanding the lessons behind the experiences!

This is your life. Don't settle for going through the motions.

SECTION I
THE FOUNDATION FOR A LIFE OF FULFILLMENT

CHAPTER 1

AWARENESS: THE ESSENTIAL PIECE

AWARENESS, DEFINED AS *the knowledge and understanding that something is happening or exists,* is the baseline to living a happy and fulfilling life. It's the foundation of everything you know and understand in life. The more aware you become, the more you can live your life as the person you are meant to be and allow yourself to experience fulfillment. People these days choose to see what things are on the surface. Out of fear, laziness, and conformity, they fail to choose to see the deeper meaning of things. I encourage you to choose to see the world anew each and every day. It's seeing the world differently through a different set of eyes. They are still your eyes, but now you choose to see things and life differently.

For example, if you have ever played sports or given a presentation or a speech, you may have gotten those proverbial butterflies in your gut prior to going up to bat or walking on stage. You are aware that you're going to get them, but you can make a choice about how they affect you. You can let those butterflies get the best of you and avoid the situation, or you can embrace that anxiety and use it to get fired up to do whatever you were nervous about in the first place. The key is to be aware that the butterflies exist and choose your reaction to them.

As you become more aware, you can't help becoming more introspective. You see the beauty in the smallest of things and the awe in the biggest of things. Or you may see the awe in the smallest of things and the beauty in the biggest of things. Awareness is powerful, freeing, and fulfilling. It causes you to want to reflect on what is and why. And by becoming aware of all that through reflection, you allow yourself to be fulfilled.

A Simple Game of Catch

Back in 2001 when former manager of the Baltimore Orioles Cal Ripken Sr. passed away, things took a funny turn for me. Cal Sr. was the father of one of the most famous, if not *the* most famous, Baltimore Oriole of all time, Cal Ripken Jr. I was listening to a radio program discussing the father-son relationship the two of them had. They discussed the closeness of the two, the special bond, and many other things. It made me think about my relationship with my father. I was saddened when I thought about never hearing my dad say "I love you" or "I am proud of you, son!" to me or any of my siblings.

My dad is an "old school" Italian. He grew up in a family where he never heard those words either. But times are different now, and I needed to know I was loved! I needed to know I was accepted by my dad! I needed to know!

One evening, while walking my dog, I was thinking about my relationship with my dad. *I am thirty-four years old and I have* never heard my father say the words "I love you, son!" or "I accept you, son!" Instead of getting angry about it, I decided I would do something nice for my dad. I thought, *What is something really special I could do for my dad for Christmas? What could I do that would be meaningful to him?* Here it was June, and I was thinking about Christmas!

When I was growing up as one of seven children, money was pretty tight. You can imagine how valuable hand-me-downs were. I will never forget the day my father walked through the door with my first baseball glove! (It was passed down to me, of course.) Wow! I was five years old and baseball was all I could think about. I was so excited! It didn't matter to me that it wasn't brand new.

While walking my dog, I was thinking, *Baseball has always been my true love, and I have never played a game of catch with my dad. Wow! What if I could give my father the first baseball glove he gave me when I was young and ask him for a game of catch for Christmas? Wouldn't that be wild?*

Before I knew it, I was obsessed with finding the glove. June, July, and August went by, and I couldn't find it. September, October, and November went by, and still no glove. I was a mess! I began to doubt my plan and why I was even pursuing it. As each day passed, I would even question God: "Why won't you let me find this glove?" I had all but given up hope. There I was, December 19, and no glove.

I woke up Dec. 20, 2001, thinking this day would be no different than any other. I headed over to my parents' house to say hello. My father was recovering from recent hernia surgery and remained restricted from lifting heavy objects. We talked and ate and talked some more. While we were sitting at the dining room table, my father asked me if I could take a box out of the basement closet. It was big and much too heavy for him. Without hesitation, I went down the steps to the closet and opened the door to find a huge box that barely fit inside the door. I squatted down, slid my hands on each side of the box, and pulled the box out of the closet. Then I noticed something on the floor that had been *under* the box.

I couldn't believe my eyes! There was the first baseball glove I ever had. The mitt my father walked into the house with that day when I was five years old and gave to me as a hand-me-down from my cousin. Twenty-nine years later, beneath the box for God knows how many years, lay my first baseball glove.

Blood rushed through my veins and tears welled up in my eyes. My Christmas wish was about to come true! I was going to play catch with my dad for the first time ever! I couldn't let my father see my emotions. If he did, he might ask what was going on, and I did not want to give away my surprise.

I asked him if I could take it. He said, "Of course, it's yours."

I left my parents' house and went directly to my home office. With my emotions running rampant, I sat down in front of my computer and wrote a poem to my dad that would forever change my life. In the lines that follow are the words that poured out of my heart that day. When I wrote these words, little did I know the impact they would have on me and so many other people with whom I would connect in the following years. This is what I wrote:

Some Catch

Hey Dad! It's Christmas time again, and families all around the world are getting ready to share their Christmas joys.

As usual, moms and dads get a list together from their little girls and boys.

Some lists include such things as cars and trucks.
While others include things like Barbie dolls and makeup.

Boys will ask for video games and sports things.
While girls may ask for dresses, clothes, and angels with little wings.

You have been a dad for thirty-six-plus years now and worked for forty-five-plus years as well.

You have had the opportunity to raise seven children, which is priceless, but I'm sure caused all kinds of hell.

I could not imagine how hard it must have been with all that weight upon your shoulders.

But I think I am beginning to understand, now that I'm much older.

Dad, we're all older now and most of us have moved away.

Now it's time for you to have some fun because we all know you've earned your pay.

If I could ask for one thing from you for Christmas, Dad, it would be . . . No, not a house, not a car, not even a watch.

All I want, Dad, is to just play some catch.

From the Heart,

Rob
December 25, 2001

We played catch for the first time ever that Christmas morning.

The Breakthrough

I was a guy in my mid-30s who was always on the go. I was frantically trying to move through my day, my life, and my business at ninety miles per hour, and yet I was going nowhere because I had my foot on the brake. Since I was eleven years old, I had been working feverishly to earn and save money. I was afraid of not having enough, and at the same time I had a low sense of self-worth. I had many insecurities, and work allowed me to hide those insecurities. One of those insecurities was the thought of not being loved and accepted by my dad.

As we were playing catch on that frigid Christmas morning, I thought, *When he throws the ball to me, he is saying, "I love you, son!" and when I throw the ball back to him and he catches it, I am hearing the words, "I accept you, son!"* For thirty-four years, I had never heard those words. Although, I did not audibly hear them that morning, I heard them loud and clear in my heart.

I gained an awareness from that experience. Once I heard those words in my heart—and believed them—I was able to take my foot off that proverbial brake and move forward in my life. I was able to embrace who I was and follow my heart's desire to be who God created me to be and not allow insecurities to hold me back again. I was able to receive my dad's love and acceptance, the only way he knew how to express them.

That was the day both of our lives changed forever. Not only did I feel loved, but my father also actually started saying the words, "*I love you, son! I accept you, son!*" I believe in my heart of hearts he felt a sense of freedom on that day as well, and we were both able to experience a sense of fulfillment.

The Impact

I shared this story with a mentor of mine, Brian Buffini, who owned a real estate and lending coaching company. He in turn shared the story of how I became aware of my insecurities and overcame them with thousands of people over the next three years, and I discovered my experience was not only a life-changing story for me, but for others as well. One man decided to find his biological mother after hearing my story; another man abandoned his workaholic tendencies in favor of a weekend skiing with his family instead, and many others told me they were inspired to improve their relationships with a parent, sibling, or friend.

In hearing my story, those people became aware of some shortcoming in their life. Have you ever felt that you are being held back from accomplishing a goal? Have you ever thought that you were on the brink of something significant, but couldn't figure out why you weren't making the big breakthrough? What held you back?

Most of us have encountered something that has held us back from becoming who we are supposed to be or doing something we feel called to do. Are you aware of what's holding you back? If you're not sure, take the time to reflect on your life and think about things you have wanted to do and haven't done. Think of some of the insecurities you may have in your own life. Do you hide them in your work? Do you hide them in another way? Ask yourself why. Think about times when you feel you are running at ninety miles per hour and have gone nowhere. Has this been a common theme for you? If so, that experience might be trying to tell you something. Dig down deep. Be transparent with yourself and discover what's holding you back.

When you are aware of what is holding you back, you can work on that to allow yourself to experience a sense of fulfillment. My hope is after reading this, you will have the courage to take action—remove your foot from your brake and live the fulfilling life you were designed to live. It all starts with awareness.

Increasing Your Awareness

So how do you increase your level of awareness? It's not as easy as you may hope. There is no formula that says, "If you do this plus that, you will gain greater awareness." Increasing your level of awareness is about being open to receiving insights through your experiences and observations.

I didn't think about how important this was until my own level of awareness increased. It first hit me one day while I was reading the book *Mere Christianity*, by C. S. Lewis. I was pretty bored with it until I reread the chapter entitled, "The Great Sin." The great sin is Pride! As I read the chapter, I was overcome by this feeling that the words on the pages were referring directly to me. I became aware of my own pridefulness. It was humbling yet encouraging. I had to take some time to reflect and really embrace this idea that my pride was holding me back from becoming more of who I was supposed to be. I began to understand who I was in my everyday thoughts and actions.

Prior to this, I believed I was better than others. I thought I knew more than other people, and no one could convince me of things other than what I believed. I was a stubborn individual. Now, in this moment of awareness, I became someone who wanted to be a better person. I wanted to be humble and kind and not think I was better than or more important than others. It became important to me to take my life to a new, deeper level.

We can choose to either stay at our current level or ascend to a higher level to become who we're supposed to be. If you choose to move to a higher level, here are some things you can do: You can read, do research on any given topic, find a mentor or a coach to guide you in a particular area of your life, and/or allow the Holy Spirit to enter your life.

Reading and doing research are easy things to do. Finding the right mentor takes a little more time and discipline. If you're a spiritual person, you can increase your awareness through quiet time and prayer.

Developing Awareness through Prayer

After being exposed to the existence of pride within me, I stumbled upon another book, *Open Heart, Open Mind*, by Thomas Keating, in which he discusses the levels of consciousness or, interpreted another way, the levels of awareness. This book was a huge stepping-stone on my journey to awareness. Keating describes how to increase your levels of awareness by centering yourself in prayer.

Keating teaches how to empty the mind of all the thoughts that flow through it on a daily basis, and how to open yourself up to new and better insights into life and about yourself. Ultimately, this leads to what is known as Contemplative Prayer. Some would call it meditation. When you free your mind of all the clutter, you allow new thoughts to enter your mind. This allows you to experience awareness on another level. It opens your heart and your mind to experience life as it was meant to be.

For six years, I practiced this method of prayer five days a week. It's a form of prayer that does not show results right away. It requires time and patience. If practiced with discipline, amazing results will come from it. (If you are interested, I highly recommend Keating's book.)

For example, I had been listening to a Wayne Dyer program while in my car. During a segment of the program his daughter Sky came out on stage to sing a song based on the prayer of St. Francis. Here is a portion of the prayer:

O divine master grant that I may
not so much seek to be consoled as to console
to be understood as to understand

To be loved as to love
For it is in giving that we receive
it is in pardoning that we are pardoned
And it's in dying that we are born to eternal life

I had heard this prayer and recited it hundreds of times since I was a child, but I never grasped the concept until this moment. I felt God was telling me something in the song, but I couldn't figure out what it was until I played it for a tenth time. Then it hit me. If I want to be loved by someone, I need to love. If I want someone to console me, I need to console others first. I became aware that I made loving others conditional on others loving and consoling me first. Now I understood I must love and console others unconditionally as part of living a fulfilling life.

I would receive insights like this and many others over the years as a result of practicing contemplative prayer.

Awareness comes to us when we least expect it. Think of moments when you are doing something and suddenly a light bulb goes on in your head, and you think, *Wow, I get that!* Or, *Wow, now I understand what is happening.* These "ah-ha" moments can't occur unless you free your mind of all the daily debris that clutters it. Are you allowing yourself quiet time to reflect and clear your mind of the clutter that blocks insights and awareness into your life?

Awareness from Parenting

Parenting is one of the most challenging tasks you will ever face. We nurture our children when they are infants, we teach them as they grow, and at times we have to push them in the right direction. At some point, our children gain a sense of independence and begin to explore things on their own. They want to make their own decisions and don't want to be told what to do.

A mistake we sometimes make as parents is wanting to live vicariously through our children. I can speak from experience on this topic. I never wanted to be the dad who lived vicariously through my children. I swore I wouldn't be. But sure enough, my son taught me a lesson on just this topic.

I have loved baseball my entire life. When I was five years old, all I wanted to do was play ball. I introduced my son, Robbie, to baseball when he was four. He fought me on it, but I forced him to play. As he grew a little older, he continued playing and for the most part I didn't have to force him to play. However, several years later he talked about not playing anymore. I responded by pushing a little harder, telling him he didn't know what he would be missing if he stopped playing. I figured I was doing the right thing. My son had some talent, and I wanted him to play. The question is, did I want him to play for him or did I want him to play for *me*?

When Robbie was fourteen years old, things started brewing. The previous summer, we had sent him to Boston for a leadership camp. While away, he went to a seminar and received a book, *The Seven Habits of Highly Effective Teens* by Sean Covey. I was excited for him, because I had read *The Seven Habits of Highly Effective People* by Stephen R. Covey, and I knew he would learn a lot from it. I didn't want to push him to read it, but I *did* want him to read it at his choosing, not mine.

One day, while we were doing something around the house, Robbie made this comment to me: He said, "Dad, I need to change my paradigm." Initially, I was caught off guard with laughter, but soon after, I realized where he had read it. The smile on my face was huge. My son had decided to pick that book up and read it. It was a blessing! I knew from reading that book Robbie would be exposed to some incredible information. If he stuck to it, he would grow immensely.

On the night of October 19, 2013, Robbie told me he had something important to discuss. I could see by his body language that he was pretty anxious about talking to me. I put my arm around him and asked, "What's going on, buddy?"

Looking down toward the floor at first, and then making eye contact with me, he responded, "Dad, you know I am not crazy about playing travel baseball anymore. I want to stop living a parent-centered life. I have to stop doing things just to make you and Mom proud of me. I need to do things that make *me* happy. I want to have fun. I must start living a principle-centered life."

With that my jaw hit the floor. I was speechless! I looked him in the eye and said, "Did you think I was going to get angry with you?"

Robbie responded, "Yes, because I know how much you want me to play baseball."

I told him there was no way I could be mad at him. I told him how proud I was of him for having the courage to come to me to have that conversation. That was a huge moment for both of us.

I'm sure my son must have been struggling with the burden of making us proud of him for a long time. At first, I beat myself up a little for conveying the message to him that he had to do something well to make us proud. Many parents are guilty of this to some degree. But I also considered how happy I was that my son had the confidence to come to me at that moment and have that conversation.

Both of us had moments of enlightenment in this encounter. Robbie was made aware of the type of life he was living by reading a simple book for teenagers. I was made aware of a message I had been conveying to my son—a message that, if not addressed in time, could have led to future issues.

Becoming Aware of Your True Self

Doing things to make our parents proud is normal as a child. But as we get older, we start doing things just to get an affirmation or an acknowledgement. As adults, we sometimes do not do what we really want for fear of what others may say or think. We act because we want to be liked, and in the process, we bury the gift of who we are supposed to be deep inside ourselves. We go on living our lives behind a mask.

Being true to yourself, or being your true-self, is an up-at-dawn, down-at-dusk task. Every day, you must get out of bed and be willing to bury your false-self and fight to be your true-self. In other words, are you doing things to get others' approval, or are you doing what you really want to do in your heart? When you can achieve this, you are truly living a life based on your own heart's desires.

I equate living a false-self life to living a life based on what others think you should do. My son taught me a valuable lesson that day, and for that I am sincerely grateful. So, I must ask myself each day, *Am I doing things to make others approve of me, or am I being true to myself? Am I doing things to be liked, or do I wish to be respected?* You can be liked because of who you are, but you may not be respected. If you are respected first for your values, people will ultimately grow to like you. In Robbie's case, I pushed hard for many years before realizing you can't force a child or any person to possess the same passion you have for any subject or endeavor. You have to let others be true to themselves.

This gift of awareness was huge for me, as I know it can be for you. It was a powerful experience to understand what had held me back from truly connecting with my son in the past. Learning how to increase my own awareness and understanding who I am have also made me a better person. I examined how often I worried about and based my actions on what others thought of my professional and my personal life. And I changed how much I weighted that in my decisions and behavior. We can all fall prey to this extremely easily. Awareness is a skill that can and should be developed over time to teach us to stop worrying about what others think, to allow new insights in our minds, and to discover all there is to know if we truly wish to become the best we can be to live a fulfilling life. There are new understandings that awareness will help us discover every day if we are willing to explore that path!

REFLECTION QUESTIONS

- Where in your life are you being held back?
- What is holding you back from being the best person you can be?
- What are some "ah-ha" moments in your life, and what did you learn from them?
- What can you do today to increase your levels of awareness?

CHAPTER 2

HUMILITY:
A DOSE OF REALITY

Humility (adjectival form: humble) *is variously seen as the act or posture of lowering oneself in relation to others, or conversely, having a clear perspective, and therefore respect, for one's place in context. In a religious context this can mean a recognition of self in relation to a* **deity** *or deities, acceptance of one's defects, and submission to* **divine grace** *or as a member of an organized, hierarchical religion. Absent a religious context, humility can still take on a moral and/or ethical dimension.*

WHAT IS IT ABOUT HUMILITY that makes us who we are? Many times when we are served a slice of "humble pie," it is because for some reason we have drifted from the center of our being. The "pie" is a reminder of who is really in control of our lives. We may have been living successful lives or coasting on easy street for a while, never giving a thought to our purpose or even giving a mere thought of gratitude for what we have. When we get away from the core of who we are, we may take for granted everything we have or everything we have accomplished. Ultimately, we may think we are the reason we have succeeded; that we are the reason we have what we have. We get "high on our hog" and forget to give credit to those who *really* deserve it. It's when we become aware of the moments of humility that we grow. Over the years, I have been humbled on many occasions, and I would love to share some of those experiences and what I have learned, and I encourage you to look at the times you have been humbled in your life and what you can learn from those experiences.

As crazy as it may sound, I do like to be humbled because I know I will learn a lesson about who I am and what I am supposed to do in this life. While the act of being humbled can hurt or taste awful, it almost always will endow you with a new awareness, and therefore it is one of the greatest gifts bestowed upon a human being.

Humility from Selfishness

God has humbled me many times over the years. It never tastes good, but I learn and grow from it. We can be humbled as a result of many experiences in life. Some of those experiences are the results of our arrogance, pride, selfishness, competitiveness, ignorance, and more.

I had been going to church for several years in the mornings after dropping my children off at school. I would get there so early that no one else was there yet. It was just God and me. I would spend close to an hour reading scripture, reading a book, journaling, and then working on contemplative prayer. For years I did this every day. If I arrived at church late and there were people inside, or if Mass was being celebrated, I would go to the basement chapel and do my thing down there. Within a few years of beginning my morning rituals, I discovered the church had completed a study that revealed the entire basement required mold remediation and subsequent renovation. I needed to find a new sanctuary. I went to the choir loft and did my best to focus, but it was tough. I did as best I could for as long as I could. It was challenging with all the people coming inside to celebrate morning Mass. So many distractions!

Then one day, when my children had a break from school, I decided to go even earlier—early enough that no one would be there. I pulled in the parking lot, got out of my car, and walked toward the church. As I opened the main door, I glanced around and to my delight no one was there! It would be just like old times. God, me, and nobody else. I was excited! No sooner had I finished the thought, God hit me right upside the head. I felt Him saying to me, "How selfish you are! You think you can have me all to yourself? There is more than enough of me to go around. Now get inside and don't worry how many people are here. I am here for everyone." Who was I to think God only wanted me to spend time with Him in church? I was humbled by this. God wants us all, and He wants us all the time. He only requires that we give Him an hour a week, and most people don't even give Him that.

In that moment, I was made aware of my own selfishness. It was a powerful moment for me. Since then, I try to recognize when I'm being selfish, and if I am, I take myself back to that day and realize there is a world of abundance all around me and there is no reason to be selfish. When I am made aware of things like this, it's not a time for me to get defensive but instead to embrace the learning moment and use it to grow going forward.

We all go through life wanting things for ourselves. It's an inherent trait of scarcity that we are all born with and have to grow out of. The problem is most of us never grow out of it. How often must we teach our children to share? For the most part, they believe everything is theirs, and we have to teach them the art of sharing. So when God spoke to me, it made me think about how often I may be selfish in my life and in my business.

Humility from Scarcity

In my business, or any business, it's possible, if not probable, for us to experience the same feelings as related to humility from selfishness in the previous story. When competing for a client and losing out on an opportunity, what feelings do I experience? Early on in business, I may have had the feeling that I just lost something, or something was just taken from me. That is a scarcity feeling. The appropriate sentiment would be to embrace the idea that the client felt there was a better match with someone else. There is always another client out there ready and willing to hire me, and I should remind myself, *"Hey, that's okay. There is enough out there for everyone."* With that attitude, I work from a place of abundance and not scarcity.

Therefore, it's humbling to accept that you are not the only one on someone's list. There are others out there who want the same thing you have and feel the same way you do. To be rejected does not always feel good. Think of the time when you were younger and maybe not the best athlete out there. You and your friends got together to play a game of ball. Two guys each picked a team, and you were the last one picked. How did you feel? It probably wasn't a good feeling at all.

When in your life or in business have you experienced similar feelings? Maybe you were assuming you were going to get a promotion at work and you were overlooked in favor of another person. When overlooked, you may have been humbled. How did you feel in the moment? What did you do to overcome those feelings? First you must embrace what happened and then understand or take the time to investigate whether or not you could have done something differently to result in a better outcome.

Or maybe that person simply had better credentials.

Understand the situation and then embrace what is, knowing your time will come.

My Arrogance Cost Me $450,000!

In March of 2000, God knocked me on my rear end financially. I was thirty-three at the time and doing very well. Ten years earlier I had graduated in 1990 from Florida Atlantic University. I had received a partial scholarship for baseball and had paid the rest out of my own pocket. So I thought I had a pretty good understanding of the value of money. I worked really hard from 1992–2000. I read hundreds of personal growth books and was as frugal as I could be. I bought small amounts of stock here and there. It was accumulating little by little until at one point I had amassed a net worth of almost $750,000. I was thirty-three years old and almost the millionaire I had dreamed to be.

I was driving down the road one evening with my wife in the car, and I was bragging a bit about how well we were doing. I even made the comment that we could sell everything we have and live pretty comfortably over the next ten to eleven years according to the lifestyle we were leading at that time. The very next morning things started to head south. I was playing the leverage game in the stock market with calls and puts (for example, if my account was worth $100,000, the firm might let me borrow as much as $50,000 to purchase more stock). I was writing naked puts, which is a dangerous game to play (but the reward is pretty good). The stock market took a little bit of a hit the next day, and so did my account. It continued to do so for the next several days. I was looking for a bounce back, so I held my position. The next week, the market continued to slide. Despite this, I remained positive with the hope that things would soon turn around. Before I knew it, I was stuck. I felt the market had dropped too much for me to sell, and now I was praying for a recovery.

The market didn't recover, and neither did my account. I knew the end was near, but I just didn't want to let go. Leverage, I thought, was the name of the game in the market. I had used the equity I had in my other positions to borrow money to buy new positions. Because the values of the stocks I was interested in buying had dipped below a certain level, I was getting margin calls—demands to sell stock I already owned to pay off some of the debt on my other positions—almost every day. Down and down the market went. Lower and lower went my net worth.

The margin calls continued to come until finally in March of 2000, I pulled into my driveway and sold my last shares of stock in my account, seven hundred shares of T. Rowe Price stock. It was the end of a nine-year relationship I had had with the stock market. We were breaking up! As much as I knew it was ending and there was nothing I could do about it, it was still the most painful day of the relationship because it became real that day. No more hope. No more, *What if I can just hold out a little longer?* It was over. I had saved so long and worked so hard to establish myself financially. I was devastated!

The best way to explain my experience was to compare it to a relationship you may have had with a boyfriend or a girl-friend when you were younger. So, everything was going great. You got along well. You loved spending time together. Everything you did, you did right. Nothing could go wrong. Then, at some point things started to change. Something would happen and you would get in a little argument but think nothing of it. You assumed you'd bounce back and everything would be okay. Things settled down, and then a week or two later another disagreement, another argument. Again, no problem, you would bounce back. Now, the arguments kept coming more frequently and the recovery time took longer. You were at a point where you knew the relationship was not going to last, but you just didn't want to let go. You were holding out for every last hope that it would work itself out until one day reality set in. The end had come, and you had to accept it, no matter how painful. The most painful day was the day you actually let go.

I was feeling that pain when I had to tell my wife a terrible truth: "Deb, we lost everything!" I thought I was smarter than I was. I thought I was invincible to a point. I put my head in my hands and broke down. God had brought me to my knees. He humbled me! My wife looked at me, put her hand on my shoulder, and said, "Don't worry about it, honey. We will be okay. I know you will bounce back. I believe in you!" Totally the opposite of what I was expecting. I feared it was going to be an all-out fight, and yes, maybe the end of our marriage. In hindsight, I learned not to take things for granted and I learned to be a more prudent investor. I learned not to be so greedy. I learned I wasn't invincible. Most importantly, I learned how much my wife believed in me! What a gift—an expensive one at that! How many people pay $450,000 to hear their wife believes in them? Not many. I sure did!

I had a choice at that point: I could beat myself up, bury my head in the sand like an ostrich, or come out swinging. In my mind, I had only one choice. For every major mistake we make in our lives, it usually takes seven years or so to recover. That's approximately what it took me. I'm happy to say it made me more focused and more determined to rebuild my finances and be more prudent. Most importantly, I wanted to prove my wife right. And I have. Since then we have recovered the losses and more.

I also learned from that experience that I'm not invincible. In that moment when I was driving down the road with my wife, I had a lot of pride. I was not only proud of what I had accomplished up until then, but I also had this feeling of invincibility, a feeling that no one could take it away from me. I was made aware that I can't do it alone in this life. God allowed me to be where I was financially back then, and He was able to take it away to teach me a valuable lesson in humility.

How can my story apply to you? Maybe you are in business with a client who has had his day in the sun. You may be in a relationship with someone special to you, going through the same painful scenario, but you just don't want to end it. You know it is not healthy to continue. You know the reality. Think it through and make the right decision. There is no removing the pain. It is going to be there, but the good news is, in time it will get better.

Reflect back on your life and think about a time when you thought you were invincible or when everything was going great and you let your guard down. You may have thought you were better than you were, and then something changed. Things started going south or falling apart. Did you acknowledge it, or assume it would pass and things would get better? Did you think you were too good for something negative to happen to you? When we are arrogant or feel we are invincible, sometimes God allows what we perceive to be negative experiences to occur in our lives to bring us back to a place of being genuine, one where we don't think we're better than we really are.

When a client puts trust in me to sell his house, it's game time. It's time to go to work and get that house sold. I have to show my clients that I am working hard to reach the goal line. Sometimes things don't work out and the house doesn't sell, and I receive that inevitable phone call. The voice on the other end says, "Rob, we are going to move in another direction." Yes, that stings a little bit. The question is, what are you going to do about it? Is there a learning moment in that humility, or are you going to play the victim? Humility is our chance to grow and an opportunity to become more of who we are created to be. It's a gift!

Humility from Taking Things for Granted

Several years ago I enrolled in swimming lessons scheduled every Wednesday morning. Yes, that's right. I did this at the age of forty-three. I got out of the pool one day, took a shower, and felt like I had water in my right ear. One thing seemed different, though; I did not have that familiar swishing sound in my head. I just couldn't hear as well in my right ear. By Friday, things were getting worse. There was no sound at all. I went to a walk-in clinic that evening, and the doctor found no water in my ear. He checked a couple other things, and he surmised I was having allergy issues and that my Eustachian tube was clogged. He gave me a nasal spray and some decongestion medicine and told me I should be fine in seven days. I began taking the medication immediately, but I didn't feel quite right. By Sunday night, I was convinced it was more than an allergy problem.

I scheduled an appointment with an ENT specialist on Tuesday morning. The specialist checked my Eustachian tube only to find it was clear. "Let's get you back for a hearing test," he suggested. Fifteen minutes later I was back in his office waiting for him to give me the results. By the expression on his face, I knew things didn't look good. He said, "You have a 100 percent hearing loss in your right ear."

Totally dumbfounded, I asked, "How could that be?" All he said was that once in a blue moon people wake up with hearing loss in an ear and never get it back. There was no specific cause. He gave me a 20–30 percent chance of getting any of my hearing back at all. A hearing aid would not help either, because there was no sound to amplify. He gave me some steroids and asked me to come back in three weeks. Wow! I felt like a bomb had just been dropped on me.

As I drove home my thoughts turned to the Lord. I asked Him for the strength to accept His will, whatever that would be. I wanted my hearing to return, and I prayed for it to happen. My focus, though, was to be able to move forward no matter what the outcome. *It could be a lot worse,* I thought. I had so much to be grateful for. I focused on what I had and not what I had lost. Being able to accept this situation was an example of humility.

For the next couple of weeks, all I could hear out of that ear was a humming noise, like the sound you hear when you are in an airplane. If I went into a restaurant, the ambient noise seemed to be spinning all around me, and I couldn't understand who was saying what. It was extremely challenging and hard to deal with, but again, all I could do was pray and take the medication. I asked for courage to deal with this, and I prayed for acceptance of God's will if this was the way it was always going to be.

Nothing changed at all for the first two weeks. About halfway through week number three, I began to hear something. It was like the static on a radio between stations. It was a crackling sound. My hope began to rise with each sound I heard, but I didn't want to get too excited about it. A day or two later more crackling, and then out of nowhere I could actually perceive what I thought might be very faint words of people speaking. The ultimate test was the phone. I recall getting on a call with my wife, Debbie, and her talking to me. I would first put the phone to my left ear and then switch it to the right. The first time I tried it, the words came loud and clear through the left ear, but when I switched the phone to the right ear, I still heard crackling. But when I focused extremely hard, I heard a faint word— but I heard a word! My spirits were lifted as I began to hear some improvement. Within the next few days the words became clearer, then louder and louder. I was hearing again, but not 100 percent.

Two days later, I went for my follow-up doctor's visit. We went into the hearing booth. I was nervous but feeling pretty good. As I waited, the assistant handed the doctor the paperwork from the test I had taken. I was sitting just outside his office door. He looked at the test results with bewilderment and said, "This can't be accurate!"

The assistant looked him right in the eyes and said, "They are what they are. He couldn't have cheated."

With that, the doctor called me in. I sat there as he reviewed the results. He took a breath and said, "Mr. Commodari, 100 percent of your hearing has returned. Consider yourself a lucky man."

I responded, "You mean blessed."

I left the office feeling like I had just won the lottery. I can't begin to tell you how grateful I was. There are so many people who go through so much more than I did, and all I could do was think about those people and pray for their strength. People lose their sight, their limbs, their family members. Others lose their jobs, their houses, and other possessions. I lost my hearing for three weeks in one ear. And I got it back!

Sometimes we assume we are always going to have something, whether it's one of our senses, enough air to breathe, or enough water to drink, but the moment we lose access to our hearing, the air we breathe, or the water we drink, we realize how valuable those things are and we express more gratitude for them. In the moment that access is taken away from us or becomes unavailable to us, we are humbled. The lesson here is not to take anything for granted. Be aware of what you have and be grateful for it. God can take away anything He wants from us, whenever He wants. He doesn't have to answer to anyone. He doesn't have to give us reasons why. God does what He does for His reasons. Whether it is something in your life, your business, or any other sphere of influence, be grateful for what you have and not resentful for what you don't have. We tend to take for granted the material things in our lives, the people, our family members, our clients, the food we eat, the water we drink, and so many other things. The list goes on.

Our Children Can Teach Us Humility Too

My favorite form of humility is when God takes the time to teach me more about who I am through my children. I feel most parents are not open to the idea of being humbled by their children. We are the parents, after all—who are our children to think they can teach us lessons? I say who are they not to? For the most part, children don't even do this with intention; it just happens.

Years ago, on a Saturday morning, my daughter took the opportunity to hit me right between the eyes with her infallibility. Somewhere along the line, my children decided they were entitled to a snack after every meal, even breakfast! My daughter Amanda asked for a snack, and my immediate response was, "Ask your mother!" Not even two seconds went by before my wonderful and quite witty daughter responded, "Daddy, why can't you make your own decisions? Why do you always tell us to ask Mom? You're the father; you make the decision!" I was floored. How dare she talk to me like that! Then I considered things and realized she was right. Every time my children asked me for something, I would always defer to my wife. I looked at her and with a big smile I said, "You know something, you are right. I do need to stop deferring to Mom, and I do need to make my own decisions. Now go get your snack; in fact, you can have two of them."

While indulging my daughter, her response made me question myself as to how often I defer decisions in my life, not just at home, but in business and personal matters. Not being able to make a decision can signify a lack of confidence. It can also result from not wanting to be wrong or not wanting to make a mistake. Life is not perfect. We are not perfect. I have heard it said before that the best way to succeed is to fail early and fail often. When we choose to do that or embrace that thought, success is right around the corner.

In that moment, Amanda brought awareness to my life. Now whenever I'm about to defer a question to someone or stall in making a decision, I think back to that moment and how important it is to show confidence in at least making a decision in the moment, whether right or wrong, and to move forward from the outcome. What decisions are you not making? Where are you procrastinating and why? When have you avoided making a decision because you feared making the wrong one? Make a decision and keep moving forward, and see how life plays out.

Apples Don't Fall Far from the Tree

Another humbling experience for me occurred about ten years ago. Up until that time I noticed that my son, Robbie, would always take forever to make a decision. It would drive me nuts. Knowing Robbie struggled with making decisions, I decided one day to put him to the test. We were in Disney World on a family vacation. He and his sister, Amanda, wanted to buy a souvenir. Amanda knew exactly what she wanted. She was in and out; she got her gift, and then it was time for us to wait for Robbie to make this "momentous" decision of what to buy with his twenty dollars. Just as I knew we would, we waited interminably. Thirty minutes later, Robbie still hadn't made a choice. At one point he said, "Dad, I don't know what to buy. What do you think I should get? Can't you just pick something out for me?" I was so frustrated at the time, as I would guess any parent would be. I looked at him and said, "You have five minutes to pick something out or else I am taking the twenty dollars back and you won't be buying anything!" Within the five minutes, he finally decided and we were on our way.

One morning not long after we returned home, I was standing in front of my bathroom cabinet and realized I couldn't read the directions on the aspirin bottle. It was time to get reading glasses. I went to Walgreens to buy inexpensive "cheaters." I tried on pair after pair after pair. I had brought my business card, and I held it in front of my eyes with the glasses on and then off again, trying not to notice any difference. It was obvious that I could see better with the glasses. Then I had to decide which pair. Two hours later I was still trying on glasses. At one point, one of the workers at the store walked by, looked at me, and said, "You're still here?" I looked at her with a big smile on my face and said, "I'm thirty-nine years old, and I am buying my first pair of glasses. I am in total denial. Leave me alone." It was then I realized where Robbie had inherited his indecision problem from. Good ole Dad! It was comical, but then the light bulb lit up! I was always giving Robbie a hard time about making decisions, and here I was taking two hours to purchase a cheap pair of glasses.

To this day, I still struggle with the decision-making process because I am afraid of making the wrong choice. I struggle with this in my business and in my daily life as well. They say a lot of times if you don't like something in someone, it is usually a reflection of something you don't like within yourself. When I take a good hard look at how I get frustrated with my son watching him struggle to make a decision, it's a reflection upon me and my own indecision.

I could go on and on and tell you story after story of how I learned more about myself from my children. It didn't always taste good, as I said earlier, but as my awareness practice continued, I began to recognize these moments as gifts.

I look upon these lessons from God and think about how I struggle with my own decision-making process to this day. When I find myself struggling, I reflect on my personal experiences and the lessons learned. Then I make my decision and whatever the outcome is, it is.

Drifting

Think about all the times you may have gotten away from the core of who you were designed to be but then something occurred that brought you back to center. Why did that happen? Because it was supposed to, my friends! God lets us do things our way, but only for so long. When we get out of alignment from the person He has designed us to be, He will make an in-course correction to set us straight or to remind us of who really is in control of our lives. The appropriate word to use here is "drift." We can easily float off course in all areas of our life. We can drift spiritually, in our family lives, our businesses, in our finances, or even in our personal goals.

Here is an example of drifting in business. I have been a real estate agent for many years now. The main focus of my business is to generate referrals. My goal is to work on deepening relationships, which leads to those referrals. I have systems set up and tasks to complete that will assist me in reaching my goal. I call these my "no matter what" plan, which is also my professional business standard. It's the standard by which I wish to conduct my business each day, week, and year. For instance, I get up every morning at five o'clock, and the first thing I do is give thanks for what I have. Then I write ten personal notes to people in my database. During the day, my plan is to have breakfast, lunch, or coffee with someone in my database, as well as call twelve people. So I do this for a period of time, and I have success, closing several deals. As I get consumed with servicing the deals under contract, I may forget to stay with—or I may intentionally not continue—the basics of my formula for success. Why? Because I may feel like I don't need to do those activities any longer. That's when pride can set in, and my pipeline dries up. A month or two down the road, I have no business.

When we drift away from the center or focus of what is most important, we get humbled. It's not a punishment, my friends. It's a gift! It's God's way of saying, "Stay focused on Me!" He is reminding us to always remember what's important, and to be aware of our tendency to drift so we can correct and get back on track. When we do that, good things happen and success follows. So, whether it's work or life outside of work, stay focused on the activities at hand, be in the present moment, and let the results take care of themselves.

REFLECTION QUESTIONS

- What, if anything, have you taken for granted in your life that you didn't realize until you either almost lost it or lost it totally?
- When in your life have you seen an idiosyncrasy in someone that frustrated you only to realize you have that same idiosyncrasy?
- In what areas of your life do you find yourself drifting the most?
- What have you done or what could you do to get back on course?

CHAPTER 3

TRANSPARENCY: IT'S OKAY TO BE YOU!

HAVE YOU READ or seen *Willy Wonka & the Chocolate Factory*? In the famous story by Roald Dahl, five golden tickets have been printed inside the wrappers of Willy Wonka's chocolate Wonka Bars. These golden tickets serve as passes to tour Willy Wonka's mysterious chocolate factory and a chance to win a lifetime supply of chocolate. So in demand are these golden tickets in the movie that finding one was worthy of a song!

As the story goes, five winners—all children—and their parental figures were brought into the secretive factory in a flurry of excitement and wall-to-wall media coverage. When they arrived inside, the guests were shown all the magical technology and fantastical rooms where the candy was made.

During their tour and without their knowledge, the children were tested time and again by Wonka's clever machinery (and his elusive spy). As the movie progressed, one by one, each child failed a test and was kicked out of the factory. Gluttony, greed, and a sense of being owed something caused each child's downfall.

In the end, Charlie Bucket was the last child standing. His prize was not merely a lifetime supply of chocolate; he was given the entire chocolate factory to run when Willy Wonka retired.

The golden ticket was each child's entry into the opportunity of a lifetime, but their success was not to be found in a wrapper. Their success was to be found in how each of them approached the incredible opportunity given to them. Throughout the story we learned that these children didn't have the internal tools to recognize their inappropriate behavior. As a result, they missed an incredible life-changing gift.

Charlie, too, was guilty of punishable behavior. He stole a gumball and he snuck off the permitted tour, causing untold damage to the factory.

But it was because of his awareness that he had done wrong—and his sincere attempt to correct his behavior—that Charlie was redeemed in the eyes of Wonka. His self-awareness was evident by his acknowledging his mistake—the theft of a gumball. By returning it without inducement, he demonstrated a unique quality. He revealed to his host that he could clearly see that he had done wrong.

Here's the irony of the story: Inside each and every one of us rests a golden ticket of sorts, but it's not to be found in slick packaging. The golden ticket is not hidden in a thick wrapper or glittering adornment. The golden ticket is transparency itself, to be used as a key to unlock the door of our hearts. When we live an inauthentic life, we lock our true-self inside and we never live the life we're supposed to live, and so we are unfulfilled. To live a fulfilling life, we need to be authentic, and to be authentic, we need to be transparent.

Transparency Is the Ticket

When we were created, we were given this key. When we feel challenged by external and internal forces acting against our true nature, all we need to do is unlock the door of our closed heart and open up to who we truly are.

The majority of us, unfortunately, seem unwilling to reach inside and turn the key. Many of us are not going to do the work of being true to ourselves and others. We'd rather stay fixed inside the personal prisons we create. When we try to be someone we're not, we lock our true-self in a cage inside our hearts. Rather than unlocking the self-awareness that frees us from our self-limiting beliefs—the beliefs that we're not good enough, smart enough, and so on—we imprison ourselves to a point where we miss the endless opportunities that keep coming our way. We are not transparent, even to ourselves.

Many of us are too busy trying to be who we're *not*. We're so busy attempting to satisfy someone else's expectations that we ignore the path to our internal freedom. So often in life, we act the way we think others want us to act. We say things based on what we believe others want to hear. There are so many outside forces playing on us every day that we come to believe that we should be like someone other than ourselves. We compare ourselves to others, and often we come out on the losing side. Then we end up competing with an unwitting opponent to reach someone else's goals, instead of trying to achieve our own.

I believe that it is an insecurity within each of us that causes us to build our personal prisons. Our insecurity prevents us from being able to look at ourselves clearly and from projecting ourselves to others in a transparent manner. We would rather not be introspective;

we would rather not reveal our misgivings about ourselves to others. Instead, we prefer to be opaque about our faults, weaknesses, and failings. Unfortunately, the longer we keep buried the key that sets us free, the longer it will take to realize who we were meant to be.

In my own life, being true to myself is an up-at-dawn, down-at-dusk task. I awake every morning and have to coach myself on that task. It is no surprise to me that I have to work at it. While growing up, it was customary in my generation for a young boy who was sad or hurting inside to not show his feelings. We had to be tough guys. If we let anyone know we were hurting, we would be considered weak. No one likes to be referred to as weak, especially a boy. I had to prove I could handle things. That is the way it was.

But in 2002, at age 34, I went to a seminar in Maui called Peak Performers, and everything changed. While there, we discussed the topic of transparency. I was sitting in a room with 250 people listening to presenter Brian Buffini, who spoke about reaching one's fullest potential. If we really wanted to be successful in life and business, he said, we could not continue to hide behind a mask.

We assume we inspire people because of our toughness or our ability to show others that nothing bothers us. In reality, however, we should be living life with the *opposite* mentality. We should reveal our vulnerabilities. That is a part of what it means to be transparent.

What Is Transparency?

The definition of transparency as defined in Webster's dictionary is the following:

Being able to be seen through; being easily noticed or understood; and also one's ability to be honest and open and not secretive.

52

When we are not transparent to ourselves or others, we are basically living a lie. We are trying to fool others into thinking we are someone or something we're really *not*. Why do we do that? Is it a matter of being fearful of not being accepted for who we are or what we believe? Perhaps we fear that being candid will be perceived by others as being insecure.

Have you ever had a friend or an acquaintance who made you uncomfortable because of his or her candor? Were you almost embarrassed to be with that person because you were afraid his or her words might offend someone? Perhaps you thought well of that person because he or she wasn't worried about what others thought. Perhaps you thought that person said whatever came to mind because he or she was covering an insecurity.

Are you confused yet? In one breath I am telling you a candid person is one who is transparent, and in the next breath I am telling you that very same person may be insecure.

There's a fine line between being transparent and being overly forward to compensate for one's fears and insecurity. The world around us is always pressuring us to be successful. To be liked, we have to act a certain way or have a certain amount of wealth. Society rewards those who take risks, and many believe that only tough people take risks.

In the United States, this balancing act plagues men, in particular, who are inundated with "tough guy" images. Men generally get caught up in one of three tough guy stereotypes. These involve the bedroom, the ball field, and the billfold.

But it takes more guts to put yourself in a position in which everyone can see you as you are. Being tough is not being courageous. Being transparent is being courageous—courageous in the sense that you are willing to be vulnerable. You have the courage to be who God created you to be and the vulnerability to allow people to see you as you are. And when you allow people to see you as you are, you are living a transparent life.

Transparency as a Parent

As a parent, it's important to me to be as open as possible for my children. More is caught than taught, as they say. Our children are too busy watching what we do, and not listening to what we say. As our children grow, we want them to be open and honest with us, but how open and honest are we with *them*?

I understand there are things our children shouldn't know or hear adults discuss. But what strikes me as a disservice is this: When our children don't hear our struggles, they grow up thinking something must be wrong with them when they encounter difficulties.

I think it is okay to let our children know when we are going through tough times. They tend to think of parents as superheroes who have no problems. Our being transparent with them is really an opportunity to lead by example, and such honesty will encourage more transparency from them.

I have made mistakes in business and in life, and I share these stories with my children. I want them to know that I do make mistakes and they are not bad people if they make mistakes too. We all have heard this, but it bears repeating—you will learn more from your mistakes than you will from your successes.

I once made a rather simple mistake in my business that cost me a fair amount of money. I had listed a house for sale with a ground rent attached to it. Ground rent means the land the house sits on is owned by someone else, and the owner of the house has to pay the landowner an annual fee, usually in the range of $150 a year, give or take, depending on the location.

The house was marketed with ground rent, but the offer was signed as if the seller owned the land. I had overlooked one small place for initials on a contract and didn't realize it until it was too late. The ground rent confusion was due to a miscommunication between me and another agent, but I had to take responsibility for my part in the error.

My sellers were anxious, and the last thing I wanted to do was to make a phone call and inform them of the error. I wanted to tell them in person, and I needed to own my part.

I called my clients and asked them if I could come over to discuss a few items. Within thirty minutes I was at their home. I explained to my clients why I was there and the mistake that had been made. I informed them that the situation would be taken care of and it would cost them nothing.

When I finished explaining everything, my clients thanked me for being transparent about the situation and also for coming to them in person and taking responsibility for the oversight. In the end, the other agent and I split the $3,500 cost of the mistake.

When one can own one's part of a mistake and be honest with others, it's much easier to be forgiven. It is also attractive to others because they now know they are dealing with a person of integrity and transparency.

The end result was a deeper level of trust between my clients and me as well as the possibility that they would tell others in the future not just of the mistake I made, but how I handled it.

Part two of the equation was telling my children about how I had made an expensive goof. We were having dinner as a family later the same evening I had visited my clients. I told them I had made a mistake and it had cost me a lot of money to rectify it. My point to them was to take ownership of an error and to be transparent about one's role. In this instance, I wanted my children to know I was willing to own up to what I had done, and I wanted them to know that they must learn to take responsibility in the future for whatever discomfort they may experience as a result of their mistakes. Doing so will deepen their relationships with people because they will not be trying to hide who they are or to blame others to cover up a problem they caused.

The most important thing for me, however, was to open a line of communication between my children and me so that when they encountered issues in their lives, they could feel safe coming to my wife and me to talk about it, and to not feel any less "human" because they made a mistake.

Children really do want to be free to be who they are, and the process starts with parents. We have a huge opportunity to give children the best gift of all—being transparent and vulnerable as good examples. If our children can continuously catch us being transparent, they will learn to feel comfortable doing the same, laying the groundwork for a life of freedom.

An Audience of One

I've been journaling on and off for about fifteen years, and I have experienced insecurities in the process. Early on, there were many times when I wrote something and then had second thoughts: *I shouldn't write this. What are others going to think when they read this?*

If I had continued to think that way, I would not have been true to myself. What I learned from journaling is I am writing for an audience of one. These are my thoughts, and I cannot worry about what others may think. My journal is the optimum place to go where I can be totally transparent.

When my journal is full, I have a small chest where I store it. The chest is unlocked, and I've let my kids know it's unlocked. They can go in the chest at any time and read what I have written. If and when they decide to peruse it, they will be able to see all the thoughts and struggles Dad experienced. They will see the highs and lows. They will see Dad for who he is or was. The most important gift I think they'll see is me in my humanness, a signal to them that it's okay to be who they are. It's okay to have struggles because that's part of life.

Being transparent allows others to see your humanness. I believe that I journal for an audience of one to leave a legacy for others.

I have attended many conferences and networking events in my professional life. Even today, I sometimes experience a sense of uneasiness when it's time to introduce myself. I am sure many people feel the same way.

When I was attending a leadership class not too long ago, the facilitator talked about what he thought was one of the best ways to make an introduction in a small environment. He shared with us the idea of writing a poem about ourselves to let everyone in the group know us at a deeper level. He gave us one sheet of paper and twenty minutes to write our poem. The title of everyone's poem was "I AM." In the interest of transparency, I am sharing my poem:

"I AM"

I am from a higher power. I choose to call Him God.

I am from all of His descendants all the way down the line to two people, Loretta & Marshall – also known as Ricky & Lucy.

I am from an Italian immigrant and a red-haired German.

I am from a family of seven children growing up initially in a two-bedroom house in Baltimore City.

I am from an age where I never heard the words "I Love You" from my father until I was 34. Therefore, I am from a lower self-esteem.

I am from a devout Catholic mother.

I am from beginning my work career at age 11 – from buying my first pair of Jack Purcels, to buying my first car at age 16, my 1969 Ford Fairlane.

I am from a competitive family because I always fought to get what was mine and keep it.

I am from paying my own tuition through high school and college.

I am from F. A. U. where I played baseball and became a man.

I am from AC/DC, Def Leppard, and Ozzy Osbourne.

Now I am from Zig Ziglar, Jim Rohn, Matt Kelly, and more.

I am from the field of dreams, the baseball field, which is my metaphor for life.

I am from the five-pound block of cheese we waited for every week or so from Social Services, when we struggled financially.

I am from a motivation to be all I can be because I attended the "school of hard knocks."

I am from being a dad at 17 to being a grandfather at the age of 43.

I am from always wanting things to be about me to now wanting things and my motivation to always be about impacting and improving the lives of others.

I am from a world of abundance, wisdom, experience, and knowledge.

I am from a fire that burns within me to reach my full potential to be all I can be.

I am from a family now of Debbie, my wife; Crystal, Robbie, and Amanda, my children; Bobby, my son-in law; and Corina, my granddaughter.

I am from being a mentor and a coach.

I am from a business owner and a real estate team of five, to an inspiring speaker to thousands.

I am from all that life is.

I am who I am . . .

Who are you?

So, who are you? Take twenty minutes or so and write your own "I AM" poem and then read it out loud. I hope it strikes a chord with you. Be willing to share who you are, and be proud of that.

Take the time to reflect and keep a journal. Write down your thoughts and feelings. Write them down for an audience of one and let the words flow from your heart to paper. Write them in a stream of consciousness, which means write down whatever comes to mind. Then reflect on your words in a quiet place. Let these words guide you on your journey in life. We have only one life to live, and that is our own. Why waste your short stay here on this beautiful earth trying to be someone or something else?

Allow yourself to be vulnerable and watch the doors open in your life. Transparency is the key! Turn the key; unlock that prison door that locks in your soul. Allow your life to happen.

REFLECTION QUESTIONS

- **What are your heart's desires?**
- **What do you feel?**
- **What do you want out of life?**
- **Who do you want to become?**
- **Are you being true to yourself? If not, what needs to change?**

Be Who You Are!

Life does not happen *to* you; it happens *because of* you. In the film *Braveheart*, Mel Gibson plays the role of Sir William Wallace. He emerges as the leader of the Scottish army who defeats the English in battle after battle. He becomes the English army's biggest nuisance, but no matter how hard they try, the English can't seem to get rid of him. In the end, Wallace is finally captured and martyred. After being sentenced to die, the King gives him a choice. He can die in a quick and simple execution by merely crying, "*Mercy*" to the king. But he doesn't. Instead, he dies a tortured death. But Wallace knew what was meaningful to him, and he led by example. Every day, he woke up willing to die for the freedom of his people, for his country, and to save his ancestral land. And his legacy is larger than life.

Okay, Wallace's commitment to his inner self may be more than most people are willing to try or will leave behind (except for our finest military members and veterans). But while being true to yourself is not supposed to be a William Wallace–level sacrifice, it *is* meant to help you achieve freedom.

So, why don't you share your true nature with everyone you meet? Do you fear being treated badly or abused in some way? With the rise of social media, that's a fair concern. There's no shortage of trolls or strangers willing to tell you how wrong you are. Their reactions could certainly serve as a deterrent.

But here's an idea: Don't engage in that kind of insecurity, and don't believe it when others malign you for being true to yourself.

This game of life is tough. There's a subtle difference between being who you are and who you're not. Being who you are comes from having self-awareness, which leads to an understanding and eventually an acceptance of yourself. So show your vulnerability where you can make a positive connection. People are more attracted to someone who is vulnerable. Others crave that authenticity. It not only allows you to be free, it opens the door for others to do the same. There's a huge opportunity!

This entire book is about me choosing to be transparent. It's my basic understanding of life and how I see it. I have thought about this for several years, and I finally put it in writing because over the last several years, I have gained even more knowledge and wisdom from introspection and self-awareness, and in my heart I know these insights are gifts meant to be shared.

Maybe it's a blessing I procrastinated writing this book. I worried too long about how others would perceive me as an author. I worried they would wonder, *Who is he to think he can impact others?* But what it comes down to is this: I reached a point where I feel that God blessed me with a way I can share with the world what I have learned in this life. My hope is that all who read this book will understand that it's *okay* to be you. By being you, you're living the life God created you to live. Look within yourself and become aware of what's going on inside you. Allow yourself to be transparent and live a life fulfilled.

REFLECTION QUESTIONS

- Where do you see yourself in this chapter?
- Are you living a transparent life or are you hiding behind a curtain?
- Are you taking advantage of the golden ticket that resides inside your soul?
- Do you have the courage to turn the key and unlock the door of your heart to be who God created you to be?

Chapter 4

ACCEPTANCE:
EMBRACING YOURSELF AND UNDERSTANDING WHO YOU ARE

FROM EARLY CHILDHOOD through our adolescent years and even as adults, we yearn to be accepted by our family, friends, and others. Why is it so important for us to be accepted? Perhaps because it leads us to a place of inner freedom and a fulfilling life. Unfortunately, being accepted or not can play a huge role in our self-worth.

People generally think of acceptance as being accepted by others, but there are two other areas of acceptance we must consider: acceptance of oneself and acceptance of others. It's paramount to learn to accept ourselves first. We must first become aware of where we are with regard to this concept. Are we even aware that we may or may not be accepting ourselves for who we are? If we can't accept ourselves, how can we expect others to accept us? And how can we expect others to accept us if we can't accept them for who *they* are?

Years ago, I wrote an affirmation: *I accept myself for who I am and for where I am on this journey in life, and accept others for who they are and where they are on their own journeys.* Acceptance of all kinds begins with a willingness to accept ourselves for who we are. When we understand our own unique gifts and abilities, it becomes much easier to have self-approval.

My Birthday Party

When I was five years old, my sister and I shared a birthday party together. She happens to be 364 days older than me. Her birthday is September 4th and mine is September 3rd, so my parents decided to have one party for the both of us. We planned the celebration and told all our neighborhood friends about it. We were both excited about our big day. When people began arriving, one person after another would come to the door, and one after another had only one gift—and the gift was for my sister. As each of these people came and I realized they were there for my sister, my heart sank lower and lower. My excitement diminished with each passing moment. Finally, one friend walked up to the porch with two gifts in her hand. I knew one had to be for me. I was finally going to receive a gift! Unfortunately, I already had the game *Chutes and Ladders*!

When the party was over, I remember my mom consoling me and telling me everything was all right. She said there was a reason some of my invited friends couldn't make the party. It still didn't make me feel any better. I felt left out and hurt. Is this experience the reason I had trouble accepting myself in my younger years? Maybe it is or maybe it isn't. I don't know for sure. What I do know is that acceptance is a choice. We all have the choice in life to accept who we are or not and to accept situations as they are—or are not.

When something like this happens to us, we tell ourselves a story. It sounds like this: *No one came to the party for me, which means no one cares about me or likes me.* That's the usual story! Is it the truth? Absolutely not! The challenge for me was to reject the story I told myself that I was of lesser value because people didn't come to the party for me. The truth is no one came to the party for me and brought me a present. That's it! If I choose to read into it any more than that, I am buying into a lie. The bigger problem is if I carry that forward in my life, then I am buying into that old pathology from childhood. I have a choice to acknowledge what was and to accept what is going forward.

You have to recognize the past for what it was. You accept that you can't change it. But you don't have to accept those same feelings, circumstances, and so on going forward. You have a choice. You can choose to be happy or you can choose to be miserable. Your choice determines the outcome. If you choose to look at the negative in everything, then you will always see the negatives. If you choose to see the good or positive in everything, then that is what you'll see. You can choose your outcomes by your attitude.

Our Upbringing Doesn't Dictate Our Future

We are all products of our environment, but we don't have to remain static. We can choose alternatives. When we were younger, we may not have had a choice of where we lived or what school we went to. But as we grow older, we can make choices that determine the course of our lives. For example, you may have lived in a poverty-stricken environment as a child, but that does not mean you have to be poor as an adult. There are plenty of stories of successful people who grew up in tough environments, but they made choices to change their future.

One of my favorite stories concerns Dr. Ben Carson, a world-famous neurosurgeon formerly at Johns Hopkins Hospital in Baltimore for almost thirty years. His story is of an African-American boy who was raised by his single mom in Detroit who went on to become a world renowned doctor. Carson's mom and dad separated when he was eight. His mom attempted suicide and suffered through depression. Life was tough. Carson couldn't change the circumstances where he was raised, but going forward, he chose not to accept a future living in those same circumstances. With the help of his mother and his faith in God, he chose a way out. Carson would study hard and read endlessly and earn his way to a better life.

He had a choice, I have a choice, and so do you. If you are not happy with where you are on your life-journey, you can decide to either accept it as it is or choose to change it. If it's not acceptable to you, do something different to change your circumstances and change your future.

For me personally, growing up in our 745-square-foot house and not having much, I knew I wanted better. The day I saw my mother pull out a coupon book to pay for goods with food stamps, I realized what I didn't want. I acknowledged where we were financially as a family because that was the reality, but I knew going forward that was unacceptable to me.

As a child, I couldn't wait until I was old enough to start delivering newspapers and start saving money to buy the things I wanted and to start saving for the future. The experience of seeing my mom use food stamps impacted me. I felt bad for my dad.

He worked extremely hard to provide for us. To be in our dire situation must have been crushing for him and my mother, but somehow we pulled through. Through faith and hard work, my mother and father were able to instill in us the lesson that if we wanted something, we had to work for it.

At eleven years old I started delivering newspapers, earning my own money for the first time. I had a morning route and an evening route. I was driven to succeed and to reach my goals. At first it was about earning money to buy what I wanted, and then when I knew I had to pay my own tuition to go to Archbishop Curley High School, a Catholic school in Baltimore City, I was driven to earn more money because now I had a responsibility as well as a goal. I was excited about being able to go to the school I wanted to attend, so getting up early and delivering the newspapers in the morning and in the afternoon didn't bother me.

Later my goal became buying my first car. When I was sixteen, I knew that if I wanted a car, I would have to pay for it myself. Again, I was driven toward that goal. It excited me to get up early because I knew I was working toward that car. I saw the future, which helped me recognize where I was and where I was going.

It's important to understand and be aware of the fact that you can't change anything about the circumstances surrounding your upbringing, whether it was where you lived or how much money your family had. Being aware of this can give you motivation and an understanding of what you need to do to better your situation in the future and live the life you desire. The question that needs to be asked is this: What are you going to change to put yourself in a better situation in the future?

Choosing Not to Accept

We can choose to acknowledge people, things, and circumstances; however, we can also choose *not* to accept. Things are what they are because of choices we've made up until a given point. We can't do anything about the past, so we must accept these prior choices for what they are. However, if we decide we want things to be better, we must choose differently going forward; thus we reject the present moment in the hopes of a better future. If I'm always coming home late from work and that causes friction with my wife and kids, that's not good. If I want to change that, I must decide that that's unacceptable moving forward and choose to be home earlier to strengthen my family relationships.

Not terribly long ago, I suffered a kidney stone episode—the most painful experience I have ever had. It was debilitating! My wife and I spent seven hours in the hospital enduring all the tests and examinations. It was a Monday, a busy day for me, but there was nothing I could do except fight through the pain. As it subsided, I reflected a bit. First, I knew I wasn't going to get up and leave. I acknowledged the fact that I was spending the day in the hospital, which meant all appointments and tasks for the day would be postponed. Second, I thought about how such a small thing could cause so much pain. My kidney stone became a metaphor for how one little mistake (if we're not careful) can have such a huge impact on others.

I had to accept I had a kidney stone and needed to do whatever necessary to pass it. However, going forward, having a kidney stone is avoidable and unacceptable. There are things I can do to prevent it—most importantly, drinking more water.

So, what's unacceptable to you right now? Reflect and think through what is going on in your life now. Is it something about your job? Are you allowing people to take advantage of your kindness, for instance? When this happens, it's a matter of self-respect. If we want to be respected, we have to change what we tolerate. What are you tolerating in your life that you shouldn't be?

Acceptance versus Resistance

Some situations are unavoidable. We can accept them and move forward, or resist and go nowhere. Years ago when I was in my early thirties, I had my newspaper distribution business. There were mornings where the weather was dreadful and I had no interest in going out to deliver the newspaper. I had eight to ten people working for me every morning who *I* expected to show up rain or shine. In poor weather, I never knew what to expect because there was always going to be someone who would come up with an excuse not to be there. I really had no choice but to acknowledge the reality of the moment. This was my business, and the newspaper had to be delivered. I could resist as much as I wanted or I could accept what it was, knowing I was going to do the job—and I was going to get soaked! It was basically a state of mind. Get out there, get the job done, recognize the circumstances, and move forward. If I chose to resist, I was going to let it affect my attitude, and essentially it would affect my entire day, not to mention my relationships with my customers.

Choosing to accept unchangeable realities in the moment brings much more peace into our lives. If we resist, the opposite is true. Why choose to be frustrated all day, every day, when you can choose peace and joy?

What gets in the way of acceptance sometimes is our stubbornness or arrogance. When we think we know better, or if we let our pride get in the way, resistance can set in. Another word for resistance is tension. In weight training, resistance is good. It helps our muscles grow. But apply that same tension in life, and we can become anxious and frustrated. Or we can be accepting and live a life of peace without tension. Your choice: tension and frustration or peace and harmony.

In Matthew Kelly's book, *Resisting Happiness*, he tells us that each morning when our alarm clock sounds, we have a choice to start our day with resistance by hitting the snooze button or with acceptance, by turning off the alarm clock, getting out of bed, and moving forward with our day. The moment we hit the snooze button we are setting the tone for the day and inviting tension and frustration into our lives.

To bring all of this back to the original topic of the acceptance of ourselves, the question remains: Do we accept ourselves for who we are and where we are in this journey of life, or do we resist the person God created us to be? We all have a purpose, a calling to be the best person God wants us to be. But He gives us free choice, and we can choose acceptance or resistance. Many of us have no idea what our calling may be, and that's part of the reason we resist. If we take a few minutes a day to quiet our minds and listen to God's voice, we will hear His calling. We must consistently do this to hear His call clearly.

Time Management

One of my favorite examples of acceptance and resistance is associated with time management. I used to get up every morning and plan. I would leave the house with my road map in place for the day. I knew where I was going and what I was doing each moment. I might be moving along during my day with everything going according to plan, and then suddenly an issue would arise that wasn't in my calendar. I would get upset and frustrated. I would resist what came my way because it wasn't what I had planned, and I would let it affect the rest of my day as I stressed out trying to squeeze in everything I had already planned.

One day as I was praying, all that changed. I remember praying the *Our Father*, the prayer Jesus taught us to pray, and when I came to the words *Thy Kingdom come, Thy will be done*, it was like God knocking on my door saying, *Hello, Rob! I have the answer to remove the frustrations from your day. All you have to do is stop resisting my plan and accept what I send your way.* It was an epiphany. If I truly wanted to do God's will, why was I fighting against what He directed to me? Once I understood the unexpected events that disrupted my plan as God asking me to do His will in the moment, then I could relax and say to myself, *Okay, Lord, this is what you want me to take care of first.* Then I was able to focus on His will, accept His plan, move forward, and do the best I could the rest of the day to accomplish what needed to be done.

I like to use the analogy of a batter in baseball. A batter looking for a fastball suddenly gets a curveball. What do coaches advise in that moment? One of three things: Go with the pitch, take it the other way, or foul it off. When I think of my plan for the day and God throwing me His curveball, I choose to go with the pitch, or as *Our Father* suggests, do His will. When I choose to do God's will, I am in a place of acceptance, and that ultimately puts me in a state of peace.

At first, this was tough for me. I resisted whatever God was sending my way. I would fight Him internally and question Him. I wanted things *my* way. But the more I was able to adjust my mindset and accept what He had in mind for me, the more peaceful my day would be. I knew all I had to do was go with His pitch, do my best, and things would work out the way they were supposed to. Actor, comedian, and writer Woody Allen said, "If you want to make God laugh, show Him your plans." Every time I feel myself wanting to do what I want to do and not accept what He desires, I think of this quote.

Next time something comes up that's not in your daily planner, pause for a moment and reflect on what is happening in that moment. You have a choice to make. Do you accept what *is*, or do you resist and create tension in your life? Ever since I had this epiphany, it has been easier for me to get through my days when the unexpected arises. Yes, I still resist at times, but when I take a moment to think about what is most important at that time and realize it must be His will, then I can move forward in peace and go on with my day.

Be Careful What You Wish For

We have all heard the axiom, "Be careful what you wish for." If we ask for patience, we can be assured there will be incidents that will test us and help us develop our patience muscle. It's like working out with weights; when you lift weights, ultimately what you're doing is tearing down your muscle tissue so that after it rests and heals, the tissue comes back stronger, thereby making your muscle stronger. When asking for patience, humility, awareness, or

74

whatever it is you're working on, there will be situations to test you, making you ask if that's what you really want.

The very morning I wrote the previous section regarding acceptance versus resistance, I was tested. I had had the procedure for my kidney stone and was supposed to get an X-ray. I could walk in without an appointment as long as I had my order from the doctor. I was supposed to get the X-ray the day before my follow-up visit with my doctor. My calendar was full, and I was trying to figure out how I was going to work in this appointment. I searched the facility hours and discovered they opened at seven o'clock. This was perfect for me. I could get in and out and be on with my day.

I pulled into the parking lot at 7:10 a.m. and could see the doors were not open yet. At 7:15, someone finally opened the doors. *No big deal*, I thought. I walked in and registered. There was one person in front of me. A few minutes later the receptionist called that person to the counter. I heard a little conversation back and forth, and then I heard the attendee mention that the X-rays didn't start until eight. I felt this rush of blood run through my veins. I wanted to lash out and ask why the website indicated the place opened at seven, yet no X-rays could be taken until eight. I had skipped breakfast to rush over there by seven, only to find out I couldn't get any services done until eight.

Immediately, I thought about what I had written earlier that same morning, "Acceptance versus Resistance." I could let myself be annoyed and lash out at the person behind the counter or I could accept the reality and go with it. If I was going to practice what I had written about earlier, I knew I had to acknowledge the situation and go with the flow.

A few minutes later, the receptionist called me to the counter to register, and I calmly let her know the website made no mention of X-rays starting at eight o'clock. I then asked if I could leave to get something to eat and not lose my place in line. She said as long as I returned before eight, I would be fine.

I left the building and drove down the street to Dunkin Donuts, hoping to find something without bread. I pulled into the drive-thru line and looked at the menu. When the woman on the other end asked what I wanted, I asked for the Brown Sugar Maple Oatmeal. The first words out of her mouth were, "We don't have the Brown Sugar Maple Oatmeal." My immediate thought was *if you don't have it, why is it on the menu?* I wanted to say those words out loud, but I remembered what I had written earlier about acceptance and resistance. I had a choice to accept what was and be at peace, or fight it and let myself get all worked up. I thought some more about it, smiled, and chose another oatmeal breakfast the woman suggested.

It's funny how God works. If you ask for something and focus on it, odds are you will be tested in ways you aren't expecting. The key is to be aware of what is happening. Fortunately, I was able to do that, and I recognized the events of the morning for the tests they were. Instead of getting frustrated and letting my day begin in negativity, I was able to remain calm and handled the situations the right way. I was then able to laugh in the moment at the thought that God was testing me. My energy was working on acceptance and resistance that morning, and I am certain He wanted to see if I was ready to practice what I was preaching.

What would you rather have in your life—resistance and stress controlling your day, or acceptance and peace? The choice is always yours. Make yourself aware of these moments when they occur in your life. You won't succeed at letting go every time—in fact, early on you will probably fail at this more often—but in time, as you continue to exercise this muscle of acceptance, you will get better at it. Eventually, you will be able to brush off potential tension with ease as if nothing ever happened.

A Foundational Part

Acceptance is a foundational part of our lives. When something happens in our lives, whether we like it or not, if we accept it in the moment, we are building the muscle. We are showing maturity in life; we are growing as individuals. In the moment, we can't change what has happened, and resistance creates tension, frustration, and instability. When this occurs, there is weakness in our foundation, and if allowed to persist, it will assure no peace in our lives.

Ultimately, acceptance is the foundation of being able to love unconditionally, and when we are able to love unconditionally, there is no judgment. If we live a life without judgment, we achieve a place of peace. Considering all the noise that surrounds us every hour, we would all love to be in this place of peace. When you sharpen your ability to accept yourself for *who* you are and *where* you are on your journey in life, and when you can accept others for *who* they are, and *where* they are on their journey in life, you will attain peace.

Once you make a choice to travel this path, the skills must be learned over time. You are not going to wake up one day and be totally competent in your ability to live in a constant state of acceptance. You will have to build this muscle over time. It will be hard at first. You will stumble and fall along the way, but as you continue to work on this consistently each day as life and God bring you opportunities to practice accepting what is, it will also become easier for you to be accepting of yourself and others.

Life is always a challenging proposition. We can make it easier by embracing what is unchangeable and by encouraging our willingness to learn. We all have an unlimited seed of potential God plants within us the day we are conceived. We have to nurture and cultivate that potential as we grow. To fulfill it, we must become aware of our unique gifts and abilities and accept them as they are. Once we do this, it's our responsibility to put them to use as God would expect us to do.

Acceptance is a choice, and the inner freedom it creates is something every individual desires, and can have. If you're willing to do the work.

REFLECTION QUESTIONS

- **Are you resisting life or accepting it?**
- **What circumstances exist in your life now that you can use to build stronger acceptance muscles?**
- **Do you accept yourself for where you are on your journey, and do you accept others for where they are on theirs?**

SECTION II

THE ACT OF LISTENING AND CREATING MOVEMENT TOWARD YOUR GOAL

LISTENING TO THE VOICE INSIDE

HAVE YOU HEARD what sounds like a humming in your heart? Have you felt someone or something speak to you, or an idea pop in your head out of nowhere? Were you excited—even fired up—at the thought of the idea? Perhaps you were thinking *this is a tremendous idea,* and you couldn't wait to get moving on the thought.

Then something happened. You began to question the idea. You doubted your ability to go through with it. You may have even challenged whether you were good enough to succeed. Finally, you decided not to pursue it at all.

That voice constantly speaks to us. Why is that? Every one of us has a voice that speaks to us. Some call it the voice of God, the Holy Spirit, your conscience, or a higher power. As I said, I like to refer to the voice as a humming in my heart. One of three things happens when the voice is speaking to you: You either don't hear it at all, you hear it but choose not to act, or you hear it and decide to take action.

Where do you think these ideas come from? Especially the good ones? They come from a higher power, and they are a gift from God. But what do we do as human beings? No sooner do we have this great idea, we do whatever we can humanly think of to defeat that idea, to sabotage it, or to put it down. We may think we're not good enough to follow through on it.

Jailbreak

Years ago I was speaking to a close friend of mine, Curtis Oakes, and we were discussing the idea of going to the "next level." He said to me, "Rob, you will go to the 'next level' in your life and in your business when you learn to trust that voice inside of you." I thought long and hard about what he said to me that day.

About a year after that conversation, an opportunity surfaced. I was asked to be the guest speaker for a Toastmasters evaluation contest. For those who are unfamiliar with Toastmasters, it is a public speaking forum, where people go to better hone their public speaking skills. I was to give a seven-minute speech, and then ten Toastmaster contestants would evaluate it. The catch was that I would be going into prison (as a guest, I might add), to give this speech to inmates who were part of a Toastmasters group inside a pre-release prison facility in Jessup, Maryland. When asked, I immediately agreed to do it, but when I walked away, I thought, *What did I just get myself involved in?*

I had a few weeks to prepare, but all I could think about was what I would say to inmates in prison. I did not want to give them any old speech. I wanted to impact these guys! Yes, they obviously did something wrong to be there, but I wanted to be an inspiration to them. I wanted to give them a message of hope. While doodling on a napkin one night, the thought came to me. The title of my speech would be "Jailbreak!" *Wow! What a great idea!* I was excited at the thought of giving these guys a message of hope with a speech titled "Jailbreak."

Only a few minutes had gone by after that energizing thought when I began to downplay it. I thought, *There is no way I can take a title like that into prison.* I figured I might cause a riot the moment I uttered the word "Jailbreak." I had visions of guards standing outside the room where I was presenting, and as soon as they would hear me say the word "Jailbreak," they would cock their rifles and initiate a good old-fashioned lockdown. At that moment I was thinking of any reason possible not to use that title for my speech.

Then my friend Curtis's words came back to me: "Rob, you will go to the next level in your life and in your business when you learn to trust that voice inside you." That was all I needed to think about. I was all in. "Jailbreak" it was!

Convinced the titled should be "Jailbreak," I was ready to move forward. I put the speech together and was ready to deliver.

On a cold and damp December morning, I pulled into the parking lot of one of the biggest and oldest prison facilities in the state. All around me were twenty-foot-high fences with razor wire from top to bottom. If an inmate was going to make an attempt to escape, he was going to get pretty bloody.

After passing through the guard gates and then through security, I entered this small room, no bigger than fifteen by fifteen feet. There were twenty inmates awaiting the presentation. We set the room up for the meeting and were ready to start. The inmate president of the club walked to the front of the room and stated the purpose of the meeting. Then he said, "Our speaker today is

Rob Commodari, and the title of his speech is 'Jailbreak.'" With that, you could see the curiosity rising in the room. Eyebrows lifted! "Jailbreak" it was!

I looked out over the audience, and in a whisper, I said, "I am planning a jailbreak! Are you in or are you out? It's a simple question. All I need is a simple answer. Are you in or are you out?" I paused for what seemed an eternity and then in a loud voice I said, "I'm not talking about the jailbreak where you climb over the fence and run for your freedom. I'm not talking about breaking through the walls or digging under the fence to gain your freedom. I'm talking about breaking down the walls that you and I and everyone in this room have inside our own heads. I am talking about breaking down the walls of fear, hate, jealousy, and anger! Now, I am going to ask you one more time. Are you in or are you out?" With that, all twenty of the guys jumped out of their seats, raising their arms, signaling they were ready to hear the plan.

Throughout the speech I made references to the movie *Shawshank Redemption*. I talked about how we were going to break those walls down using hope as our tool. I compared inmates being institutionalized on the inside of prison to how we, common men, are just as institutionalized on the outside. When inmates first enter prison, they fear those walls inside. After some time has passed, they get somewhat used to those walls. Finally, as more time goes by, inmates begin to rely on those walls to get through their day. In that same way, when given a new challenge or faced with change, most everyone will sense fear building in his or her mind. So, day in and day out, we have this anxiety regarding fear. After some time passes, we get used to fear. And finally, as more time expires, we begin to depend on fear to get us through our day. Thus, we are institutionalized in our minds by our own fears.

I concluded with the vision of the guys getting out of jail the next morning and walking toward the entrance to their freedom. I wanted them to think about their last night in prison and the long walk down the corridor toward the exit doors. Going to bed that night, I wanted them to hear that jail cell door slam shut and think to themselves, *I am never going to hear that noise again.* I wanted them to envision that walk down the corridor hearing the echoes of the guards' shoes, *click clack, click clack,* and think, *I am never going to hear that noise again.* As they were approaching the door, they were to envision taking their last step out of jail, and as they did, they were to look up to the heavens, take a deep breath, and ask themselves one final question: *Do I get busy living or do I get busy dying?*

I ended the speech right there. All twenty guys jumped out of their seats hooting and hollering! It was a total success! I connected with these guys, and I could feel it.

During the next part of the meeting, ten members were to evaluate the speech. The ten guys were asked to exit the room and enter the room next door where they could gather their thoughts before giving their evaluations. No sooner had they left when another inmate, not part of our group, came running down the hall with a bloody mouth. Lockdown time! For the next forty-five minutes, the ten members remained in the adjacent room while I waited in the presentation room. At first I was nervous, but after a few minutes I began talking to the guys still in my room. From our conversations, I learned their stories—why each one of them was there and what their background was. I was very much at ease now, and it was obvious they were too.

The lockdown eventually ended, and we continued with the planned evaluations. One by one they gave their evaluations.

As the final participant stood to give his evaluation, he looked directly at me and said, "Mr. Rob, thank you for coming here today! Thank you so much for making us feel comfortable, and thank you for looking like you were comfortable as well. Please don't get mad at me for what I am about to say, but if I didn't know any better, I would have thought you were one of us!" With that, all the inmates broke out in laughter, as did I. I knew in my heart it was a success.

I looked at the gentleman and said, "Thank you for that compliment. All you are telling me is I connected with you, and that's what I came here to do."

When I left the prison, I knew I left the guys with a feeling of hope. Hope that one day after they got out of prison, they could live a life free of fear, hate, jealousy, and anger. As I pulled out of the parking lot, I looked in the rearview mirror at the large fence with all the razor wire around it. I knew something magical had occurred. I could feel the spirit within me.

That would not have happened if I hadn't moved forward with the title. The entire dynamic of the speech would have changed. I had listened to my inner voice. From the response I received from the inmates, I gained a confidence and a knowing that when my instincts are talking to me, I need to follow them. Good things will come of it.

Are You Listening to That Voice?

The voice I'm referring to is always there. It speaks to us at home.

It speaks to us in our daily travels, in our activities, and every time we have to make a decision. We can recognize the voice by the energy or excitement we feel in our hearts. It's that humming we feel.

That voice is speaking to us all the time, but sometimes we choose not to listen.

That voice speaks to us in our work as well. It might be telling you to make a big business decision; maybe to start a new product line, build a team, or even buy another business. The voice may even be telling you to get out of the business you're in. Where in your business has this occurred for you? Did you ignore the voice or did you take action?

To help make that decision, we have to create an environment that allows us to hear that voice in our hearts. We have so many distractions in our lives, how do we tune them out? By making time to contemplate and reflect, we allow the good thoughts to enter our minds and hearts.

In the earlier "Jailbreak" story, I was aware of the voice speaking to me and I took action. Many times in our lives we don't bother to hear the voice, and if we do, we ignore it for fear of failure. When you hear the voice calling, it's hard to trust it, until you have done it a few times. Trust is a big thing, and trusting God is probably the hardest thing in the world for us to do. Luckily, God provides opportunities for us to practice doing this, too. In fact, God taught me a big lesson just a few years ago in terms of trusting Him.

REFLECTION QUESTIONS

- How often is the voice speaking to you, and you disregard it?
- Can you count the number of times in your life you have heard a calling and because you lived in fear, you chose not to take action?
- How many people could you inspire by taking action?
- If you did so and failed, would that be a bad thing?

How Swimming Led to Trust

As a child, I never liked swimming. In fact, I was afraid of the water, or more specifically, I was afraid of drowning when I got into the water. I took swimming lessons one summer as a child and I hated it. Over the years, I never really learned how to swim. I could do the doggie paddle and I could swim underwater, but I could never get the art of the swimming stroke down or the rhythm of breathing while swimming.

Over the years, I would watch my children participate on the swim team. As we sat at the pool on hot summer days, I would watch people casually and gracefully swim from one end of the pool to the other. I thought, *How hard could this really be? I can do this!*

In 2009, I decided it was time to take swimming lessons. I sat at my computer one afternoon, logged in online, and began filling out an application for lessons at a local junior college. When I completed the application, I looked it over and suddenly had a panic attack! *Once I hit this submit button, this becomes real,* I thought. I couldn't bring myself to submit the application. I turned off my computer and left for the day, trying to convince myself I'd submit it tomorrow. The next afternoon I tried again, only to suffer the same anxiety. The thought of taking swimming lessons and the fear of having to commit to getting in the water were overwhelming. On day three, I filled out the application again. I stared at it for what seemed like an eternity, and after taking a few deep breaths, I finally submitted the application. A weight had been lifted from my shoulders! Essentially, I had achieved my goal of filling out an application to go back to college to take Swimming 101. Now it was official! It was time to swim!

I had three objectives in wanting to take the swimming lessons. First and obviously, I wanted to learn how to swim. I wanted to be able to gracefully and effortlessly swim across the pool. I wanted to get some exercise in the process, and I wanted to overcome my fear of the water.

I heard Jim Rohn, a self-help/personal growth author who recently passed, say a long time ago, "Set a goal for what it will make of you." I was in for a surprise! I had no idea what was going to transpire over the next four months. It turned out to be a spiritual experience for me.

But in the moment, my enthusiasm quickly turned to panic. I was forty-two years old at the time and not only was I going back to college, I was going to learn how to swim. *Who would be in my class? How silly would I look?* This feeling of insecurity swept over me. I'm older, Italian, and oh my God, I'm hairy! In fact, they used to call me Magilla Gorilla when I was younger.

On the first day of class, I pulled into the parking lot of Essex Community College feeling like it was my first day of college all over again. I walked to the gym and then into the locker room. Feeling the butterflies inside, I continued to ready myself for swim class. Dressed in my new bathing suit and my shirt, I entered the swimming area. It was hot and humid, and there were about twenty people sitting on a bench against the far wall waiting for roll call. To my surprise, there were people of all ages. There was the young group I expected to be there. There were a few people my age, and the biggest surprise of all was the older group—at least a half a dozen people older than me. I felt much better now.

Our teacher placed us in three groups: beginner, intermediate, and expert (she didn't have to tell me where to go). I, along with five or six other students, was in the shallow end. Our teacher explained what she wanted us to do to see what our skill level was. Our instructions were to tread water first for ten to twenty seconds. Then we were to push off the wall and swim a few yards to see what kind of stroke we had and how well we breathed while swimming.

Now I'm a guy who, for as long as I can remember, gets out of bed every morning like a bat out of hell trying to get my day going. I frantically run around all over the place getting things together, planning my schedule, working out, and so forth. Everything is always rushed.

It was my turn to show what I could do. I treaded water for ten seconds or so. *It seemed like an eternity.* My arms and legs were all over the place trying to keep my head above water. When my time was up, I pushed off the wall and swam a few yards ahead, kicking frantically, my head totally above water, arms flying everywhere. It was a sight to see.

When we were all finished, our teacher evaluated us. She looked at me and said, "Rob, you were all over the place. Your arms were flying, your legs exerting way too much energy. You came off that wall frantically looking like a crazy man. You need to slow it down. You need to let the water become your friend. You need to let it come to you and relax a bit."

In that moment a light bulb lit up in my head. I looked at her and said, "That is so profound, what you said. If I could let this thing come to me, if I could let the water be my friend, if I could relax a bit, I would obviously be a better swimmer. I would also be a better husband, father, business owner, and an overall better person. And if I couldn't get this swimming thing down, at least the enthusiasm of wanting to would make me a better person." She looked at me like I had five heads. I told her not to worry but to know she had really helped me have a breakthrough.

For the next six weeks or so, my goal was to learn to relax in the water and let swimming come to me. What excited me the most was that I was going to use this as a metaphor to learn to let this thing we call "life" come to me also. It was as if I had had a baptismal renewal. I couldn't wait to get in the pool every day. It was that exciting to me! So, whereas my goal at first was to learn how to overcome my fear of the water, now it was to learn how to let life come to me.

The baseball season had started during the semester, and being a huge Baltimore Orioles' fan, I wanted to watch as many games as possible. After an Orioles' victory one evening, the broadcaster was interviewing their winning pitcher, David Hernandez. He was a rookie pitcher, and this was his first start. The broadcaster asked David this question: "What was your game plan for tonight's game?"

David responded, "I wanted to throw my pitches, hit my spots, and then I wanted to *let the game come to me.*" *Wow!* I thought. That's exactly what my swimming instructor had said about the water and swimming. "Learn to let it come to you."

A few weeks later, while I was watching the pre-race interviews for the Indianapolis 500, Danica Patrick was being interviewed. The interviewer asked Danica, "What are your goals for the race?"

Danica responded, "I want to be in and out of the pits in good time. I want to hit my marks on the track, and then I want to *let the race come to me.*" There it was again—*let it come to you.* I was so in tune with what my teacher meant when she said, "Let the water be your friend and let it come to you." I was on fire now!

The semester was about to come to an end. One day while I was swimming laps, the next light bulb lit up. I was working on my backstroke, which I despised. I wasn't a fast swimmer, so I would always take my time moving through the water. The pool was twenty-five yards long. It started as shallow water, then got deeper in the middle, and then got shallow again. As I was entering the deep part, a young guy went flying by me, causing water to splash onto my face and in my mouth. I stopped dead in my tracks, coughing and choking on the water, trying to maintain my composure. I began to tread water right while I was telling myself, *Don't panic, don't panic!*

While treading water for the next ten to fifteen seconds, *BAM*, the next light bulb lit up. I thought to myself, *If I were to go down right here, right now, who would jump in and save me? The lifeguard, of course! Well, if I were to go down in life; if I were to try something in life and begin failing at it, who might jump in and save me? God or a higher power, if you choose to call it that. Wow! What a crazy way to be taught how to trust.*

All I wanted to do when I signed up for swimming was to learn how to swim, get some exercise, and overcome my fear of the water. That first set of goals led to learning how to let things come to me in life, and it ended with God teaching me to let go and *trust* Him. What a powerful lesson!

As I mentioned before, Jim Rohn said, "Set a goal for what it will make of you." You may not know what setting a goal will make of you at the time you set the goal. You don't know exactly where the goal is going to lead you. But if you embrace the journey and listen to that voice inside, I do know it will be a hell of a ride and much will be learned along the way.

Become aware of the voice that hums in your heart; the voice that calls you to your purpose. Allowing yourself quiet time or time for meditation are good ways to clear the junk out of your head and allow that voice to be heard. You'll know it's talking to you when you feel the energy moving through your body; when you think about whatever the idea is that came to you. You will get excited and feel uncomfortable, and then you will question yourself or your ability to follow through. When you hear it, listen to it, take action, be willing to embrace the journey, and be excited as to where you will go. Most importantly, learn to trust the voice because, more than likely, it's coming from God, and He only brings good things to our lives.

REFLECTION QUESTIONS

- Is there a job, an idea, or a calling that you think about constantly? And when you do, do you feel your energy level rise? If so, explain in more detail.
- What's the worst thing that could happen to you if you decided to trust the voice inside? What's the best?
- Are you making this life about yourself or others? Explain how.

CHAPTER 6

CREATING MOMENTUM ON YOUR PATH

THE 2017 SUPER BOWL slated the Atlanta Falcons, in their second Super Bowl appearance, against the New England Patriots, playing in their seventh Super Bowl. The game was staged to be a high-scoring game with what may have been the top two offenses in the league. That said, the first quarter ended with the score being tied at 0-0. Not the high-scoring affair everyone anticipated. That would soon change.

Atlanta scored first and took a 7-0 lead early in the second quarter. They scored again five minutes later to lead 14-0. New England was not playing up to their standard, and all the momentum was going the Falcons' way. On the Patriots' next drive, Quarterback Tom Brady began moving the ball downfield. He had put the Patriots in a position to score. They were driving in for a touchdown as Brady dropped back to pass. Robert Alford of the Atlanta Falcons intercepted the pass and ran it back eighty-two yards for a touchdown. Atlanta was up 21-0, and many thought the game was over. How could Atlanta lose now?

BETTER THAN YOU THINK

They were the highest-scoring offense in the league and were leading 21-0.

New England got the ball back with a few minutes remaining in the first half and went down the field to score a field goal, cutting the lead to 21-3 going into halftime. Atlanta was going to receive the ball at the start of the second half with a 21-3 lead and all the momentum going their way. As they went into halftime, I said to a friend of mine, "The worst thing that could happen for Atlanta right now would be for them to come out in the second half and go three and out to begin the half." To me, that would mean a shift in momentum. New England did hold Atlanta on the first series of the second half, but that's not where the momentum shifted.

New England had a quick series to punt the ball back to Atlanta, and Atlanta scored a touchdown on that possession. However, those would be the last points Atlanta would score for the remainder of the game. Atlanta kicked the ball off to New England following that touchdown, and the rest is history. When New England was able to score on their next possession and hold Atlanta on theirs, that's when the momentum shifted. New England made an amazing comeback to tie the score late in the game. They gained the momentum early in the third quarter, never to lose it throughout the remainder of the game. Late in the fourth quarter, Atlanta had a chance to put the game away. They had a big offensive play, only to be derailed on consecutive penalties and a sack. Once New England tied the score, there was nothing Atlanta could do to stop the momentum. On the first series in overtime, New England took the ball directly downfield and scored the final touchdown to win the Super Bowl.

Momentum is critical in life! Merriam-Webster defines it as: *strength or force gained by motion or by a series of events.* You're either growing or dying! What you have to be aware of is that you can't stay still. If you remain still, you start to wither and you can't grow, and momentum can work in a negative way. If that starts, you have to work twice as hard to get momentum moving back in the right direction again. To grow, you have to continue moving forward, and as you move forward and see little successes along the way, you gain energy and confidence. Little by little, you make progress in bigger chunks.

A Shift in Momentum for Me

Momentum can happen in an instant, an hour, a day, or at any moment you choose to recognize it and use it to your advantage. My favorite story goes back to when I started reading books again after college. At first, as a young graduate working at an investment company, I was so sick of school that I had promised myself I would never pick up another book to read ever again. Then one morning I walked into the office and saw *The Greatest Salesman in the World* by Og Mandino lying on my coworker's desk. I asked him about the book, and he encouraged me to read it. He said it changed his life. Never having sold anything before, I decided to read it.

That was the beginning of a huge shift in momentum in my life. Not only did I read that book, but over the last twenty-seven years, I have read over eight hundred books. What I want to share with you is the momentum it created in a very short period of time and the feeling I had as a result. When you recognize momentum building, there is a certain energy you feel; there is a confidence that creates a desire to cause you to want to keep moving forward.

Momentum and confidence go hand in hand. You can't have one without the other.

I read that first book by Og Mandino, and then his second and third books. I purchased and read all the books he had ever written. I was in a reading zone. Any chance I had to read, I was going to read. I looked forward to it, and I didn't want this feeling to go away. The more I read, the more I *wanted* to read. I was exposed to this mindset that gave me a confidence and understanding of life.

What started out as a slow-moving freight train not even wanting to entertain the idea of reading had turned into a steaming locomotive that couldn't be stopped. I went to bed at night looking forward to waking up the next morning, excited to experience life. When the alarm clock sounded in the morning, I awoke excited for my feet to hit the floor and get going. For seven years I read every day; I was obsessed with reading and learning.

I had momentum working in my favor, and I had the confidence that whatever I did was the right thing to do. Everything was going to work out just the way I desired. Then the day arrived when I decided I needed to take a break from all the reading and studying. I needed to apply everything I had learned. Instead of continuing to read and study while I applied what I learned, I stopped reading altogether for a couple of years. But instead of applying the lessons I'd learned from all those books, I broke any momentum I had and fell easily into the trap of working all the time instead. When you have momentum on your side and everything is going your way, you should *not* do anything to change that forward motion.

REFLECTION QUESTIONS

- **Where was momentum created when you didn't expect it?**
- **Where did it show up when you were expecting it?**
- **Where do you desire momentum to show up for you in the future?**

Negative Momentum

Momentum can work against you, too. If a situation or two goes wrong for you, the way you begin to think could determine whether or not things continue to work against you. For instance, if you start looking for things to go wrong, guess what? They will. The way you talk to yourself can also create a shift in momentum. If you convince yourself things are not going to work out the way you desire, they won't. It's called self-sabotaging. We can induce negative momentum.

In my real estate business, there are times when I get on a significant roll receiving referrals and putting deals together. I might say to myself, *This can't continue.* As soon as I think that thought, I can cause a shift in momentum in the business. There are also times during the year when I don't get hired for a couple listings in a row, and suddenly I start going into listing appointments thinking *I'm probably not going to get this listing.* I may not get listings for the next several appointments because I created negative momentum.

Where are you creating negative momentum in your life? Are you getting up in the morning with an attitude that it's going to be a bad day? Are you going to work with the feeling that you can't wait to get home because you don't like being there? You are self-sabotaging. Perhaps you are on a healthy eating schedule six days a week. Then you decide one week you only need to eat healthy five days. You don't notice a change, so you do that for a week or two and then decide you only have to eat healthy four days a week. You are creating negative momentum, and then it becomes tougher to swing the momentum back to being positive.

Whether you are in a cycle of positive momentum or negative momentum, it only takes a small tweak in either direction to make things change for you. You may feel helpless to stop negative momentum, but all you need to do is maybe read a book, do something kind for someone else, engage in a good conversation with someone close to you, or something else that seems insignificant but still causes a slight shift. In the past, if I was feeling down or felt I needed a hug, I would seek out someone to hug. I discovered doing such an act of kindness helps create a positive feeling, which can create a positive shift in momentum.

If you have positive momentum on your side, be careful not to ease off in your effort. I often say, "When you feel momentum on your side, push on the gas harder." It only takes one bad decision, or the buying-in of one negative thought, to start to swing the pendulum in the wrong direction.

Look for opportunities in any of the spheres of influence in your life to create momentum, and you will find them. Expanding your view will expand opportunities to increase momentum in your life. You will realize there is no limit to what you can accomplish.

Building and Maintaining Momentum

From the positive standpoint, I was in the business for about a year when I decided to hire a business coaching company to help me. I began working with a company now known as Buffini and Company. The basic action steps were to write notes, make calls, and go see people face to face. The first three months I did this I was receiving very few referrals. I felt like I was doing all this work and nothing was happening. I shared my frustration on a conference call one day with the owner of the company, telling him I had followed the plan and wasn't seeing any results. He told me to continue my plan of action and eventually the dam was going to break.

What I was doing during those first three months was building momentum in how to build relationships and receive referrals. Sure enough, within the next month or so, the referrals began flowing and my business was off to a tremendous start. I had harnessed the massive energy of momentum working in my favor. I went from doing nineteen transactions my first year with no systems in place to doing forty-two my second year with the help of Buffini and Company and the momentum they helped me create with the guidance they gave me and the systems we built.

A common aspect of the real estate business is the up-and-down waves of clients. Agents will begin with no business and then will prospect hard for a period of time to generate some referrals. When the referrals begin to flow in, agents become so involved servicing the clients that they allow their energy to slip away from lead-generating. This kills any momentum built up in the prospecting phase.

Once agents have success generating referrals, they must keep doing what they are doing to generate more leads. There has to be a consistency with the time invested in prospecting. It's important to prioritize one's time to always ensure the focus remains on the prospecting so the momentum continues in the right direction. Once we take our foot off the accelerator, we lose momentum and have to start over again, creating another round of energetic prospecting to kick-start the flow of referrals back to our business.

Dr. Robert Maurer gives us an example of how to build momentum in his book, *The Kaizen Way*. He discusses how achieving your dreams and goals starts with one small step. Dr. Maurer shares a story of a client he worked with who needed to begin an exercise program. She was carrying extra weight and was overwhelmed with her work. A single mom, working constantly, while trying to support her family, he didn't want to undermine her momentum with too big of a program. He started by encouraging her to march in front of her television for only one minute every day for a week or so.

The Kaizen Way encourages us to take small steps to achieve your goals. Say you haven't exercised in years. You're overweight and out of shape. You can't seem to find the time to work out, so why even try? Well, for starters, maybe you can go to the gym and stand on the treadmill for a minute each day. Just stand there! That's it. Then week two, you walk for a minute or two each day. Now you have some momentum building. Your attitude about exercise is starting to change, and you see the possibility of improving your health. Within the next week or two, you are walking on the treadmill for five minutes a day until you build up to twenty minutes. It's all about being intentional and dedicated to achieving what you want.

In the above scenario, you are able to create momentum—however gradual. Any time you set out on a new endeavor or want to achieve a new goal, the main focus is to get momentum on your side. Once you do that, there is no telling how far you can go.

REFLECTION QUESTIONS

- **Where else are you creating momentum in your life?**
- **Where would you like to see more positive momentum in your life?**
- **What is one small thing you can do to start building positive momentum?**

Consistency Is the Key

Anytime we initiate a new activity, we spend more energy earlier in the process because that's where it is needed most. Let's take, for example, the writing of this book. I had been inconsistent for years in starting and stopping with the process. I would write for a week or two, and then I would stop. There was no consistency with the time I was investing into it. Every time I gained a little momentum and then stopped, I had to start all over again. Finally, on January 1, 2017, I made a commitment to create a consistent writing schedule. I decided I was going to get up at the same time every day and write for approximately the same amount of time each day. In doing this, I created momentum and didn't want to stop. I began to see this book taking shape, and it gave me confidence to see it through to completion.

I remember when I started journaling in 2003. I received a journal at a seminar with the instruction to write my thoughts in it every day. I was to write what I did, what I thought, and how I felt. What first started as lists soon turned into a coherent piece of free-flowing thoughts from my mind to paper. I knew from my reading that it usually takes twenty-one days of doing something consistently to form a habit. Early in the process, there were days I just didn't feel like doing it. In those moments, I opened my journal anyway and wrote something like this: *I don't feel like writing today.* Writing something that simple allowed me to keep the momentum going and not lose sight of the goal I had set to achieve.

Confidence from Momentum

We have the ability to create a cycle of ever-increasing confidence. It's not just something we receive or something that suddenly impacts us, granting us confidence. It's about making decisions and *committing* to those decisions. The first decision is to get off the fence and commit. You are going to make mistakes along the way. Accept your errors and be willing to learn from them. Now you have lessons you've learned. You value the experience, and that builds confidence. As you continue to make decisions and learn from your mistakes, you will have a better understanding of how the confidence makes you stronger. As you gain confidence, you will build momentum in whatever it is you are attempting to accomplish.

Mistakes are part of the process, and you cannot make progress without them. Embracing your mistakes and learning from the experiences are critical to building confidence. The experiences you have will provide you with your only true source of irrefutable knowledge. Confidence and momentum go hand in hand. You can't have one without the other.

Momentum creates confidence, and confidence leads to more momentum—a self-perpetuating cycle. You may have anxiety about trying something new, such as implementing a system at work or parenting a certain way at home. For me, I remember introducing the concept of doing affirmations with my children on the way to school in the morning. I thought, *My kids are going to think I'm weird doing affirmations with them.* On the way to school we said three affirmations each morning and then told each other three things we were grateful for. At first it was uncomfortable for me—and for them as well; my children Robbie and Amanda didn't know what to say. They would take their lead from me, but they still weren't sure. As time went on, they were more comfortable saying affirmations and thinking of new ones. There were even times when we got in the car and they asked me to start with them.

As you can see, something that first seemed uncomfortable became comfortable after my children accepted it and remained consistent with it. They gained confidence, then momentum. This is a small example, but my point in sharing this story is to dispel the idea that momentum and confidence must be part of a bigger outcome. We can create momentum and confidence even in the smallest areas in our lives, and we may not even realize it when it happens.

Another example for me, and I'm certain for many others, is the issue of exercising. A few years ago, I had surgery on my shoulder. I had worked and exercised with weights and have cardio trained since 1985, and I considered myself a healthy person. However, after having surgery and not being able to work out much with the weights, I found myself falling out of shape. I wasn't eating well and fell into this lazy trap of not exercising at all. When I had my blood drawn in November of 2014, I discovered my numbers were high—high enough to cause concern. I had never been on medication for cholesterol, or blood pressure, or anything like that and I didn't want to start. My weight had escalated to 204 pounds. I didn't feel good.

Following tradition at the beginning of the year, I made a New Year's resolution. I wanted this to be more than a three-week resolution, which is normally the case for most people. I had no intention of falling into that group. I made a decision to get back in shape and resume eating well. Diabetes runs in my family, and it scared and concerned me.

My goal was to drop my weight to 187 pounds by the end of 2015. I stopped eating by eight thirty each evening and gave up sweets and bread Monday through Friday. The last commitment I made was to get on the elliptical every day for at least twenty minutes. While on the elliptical, I read as well.

As with any goal, the earliest steps are the toughest and results are not immediately apparent. I got through the first week in good shape but no real weight loss. Within the next week, I lost a little more than a pound. It was tough to stay disciplined because in my mind, I wasn't seeing the weight drop quickly enough, and the temptation existed to eat bread and sweets. Then, throughout the next few weeks, I began to lose more weight. Seeing results gave me resolve to continue what I was doing. Momentum was building. As the weeks went by, my energy level improved. I began running for several miles with my wife once a week and I lost more weight. People began to notice as well, complimenting me on my progress. On May 19, 2015, I weighed exactly 187 pounds.

I lost seventeen pounds in five months. People I hadn't seen frequently asked me what diet I was on, and I would respond, "The discipline diet."

When you set a goal to lose a certain amount of weight, or to run a marathon, or to do something that takes some time to accomplish, the idea is to create momentum moving in the right direction. Once you see the momentum working in your favor, it gives you more energy and confidence to continue moving forward, which creates more momentum, and ultimately leads to achieving your goal.

Courage

Many times the thing that holds us back from creating a positive shift in momentum is the courage to commit to a decision to make a change. Life is a journey, and on this journey we are going to experience all kinds of challenges. You can let the challenges take you down the road of negativity, or you can step up, embrace those obstacles, and keep moving forward. I love the word "courage." Courage is defined as moving forward despite the fear. Fear stares at us every day. We can choose to let it paralyze us, or we can use it as a launching pad to move on to the next phase of our journey. I'm a guy who suffers from paralysis by analysis. I want everything to be perfect before I make a decision to commit to something. We all know nothing is perfect, and neither is any decision. We have to be willing to move forward despite our fear or anxiety prior to making a decision; otherwise, we will become mired in the swamp of indecision as opportunities pass us by.

I recently went to an event in San Diego called "Peak Experience." It's an annual event where approximately five hundred real estate agents get together for a personal growth experience. The theme of the most recent Peak Experience was wrapped around *The Wizard of Oz*. To get prepared for the event, we were asked to watch the movie. I hadn't watched that movie in at least thirty-five years or so. When I had watched it as a child, I thought the Scarecrow, the Tin Man, and the Lion all went to Emerald City to get their respective brain, heart, and courage. Of course, I understood as a child that Dorothy had to go to Emerald City in order to find her way home. But, as an adult, the moral of the story really hit home for me: There had been no need to go to Emerald City because all the characters already possessed what they needed—all within each one of them.

I identified most closely with the lion. I have been blessed with so much in my life, but sometimes I struggle with mustering the courage to move forward on actions or to make tough decisions. We all have a fear of something in our lives, and courage is all about facing that fear and moving forward.

All of us seek what we think we need or is missing from ourselves, but the reality is we probably lack very little. The resources we need already reside within us. Our task is to develop and extract the necessary traits, which in and of itself takes courage. When we do this, we are free to be who we were created to be. We only need to dig down deep into ourselves to find what's missing.

Seize the Day!

Several guest speakers spoke at the event, and each one had a specific topic to discuss. I led a small group discussion at lunch with about ten people. I had a list of prepared questions, but when I lead a group for the first time, I like to open with an ice-breaker question. So I asked everyone at the table, "What would you do if you were invisible?"

I asked that question because if we were invisible, how fearless would we be?

As a leader, it's proper to go first when answering a question. My answer to the question was that I like to think that if I were invisible, I would go up to everyone I saw every day and whisper in their ear, "You can do this! You can do this! You can do anything you want in life."

I imagine that as I whisper in each person's ear, it would be fun to watch them turn their heads quickly and say, "Who was that?" or "What did you say?" They would then be jolted into action by some seemingly subconscious thought that was in fact me.

Ironically, in the morning session of day two of the seminar, author Brian Moran, who wrote *The 12 Week Year*, spoke for about ninety minutes. Toward the end of his session he discussed how condensing your yearly goals into twelve-week increments forces you to be hyper-focused and present in every moment.

BETTER THAN YOU THINK

He then showed us a movie clip of Robin Williams from the movie *Dead Poets Society*. It was the scene where Williams encourages his students to follow him to the hallway outside the classroom. There, he asks the students to look at the wall of all the boys who had been through the school in the past and all the awards they received. He explains how those on the wall who accomplished so much are no different than the boys standing there looking at the wall. These celebrated achievers ate the same way, wore their clothes the same way, and did many other things just the same way the students standing there do.

Williams then asks the boys to move closer to the wall, and as they do, he proceeds to whisper in each student's ear, "Carpe Diem! Carpe Diem!" (which means "Seize the day!" in Latin).

Suddenly, watching that scene, I was filled with emotion. I thought about my answer to the ice-breaker question the day before. I saw myself as Robin Williams whispering in the boys' ears, and then I saw myself as one of the students and Williams whispering in my ear, "Carpe Diem!"

It made me think that if I were that invisible person I described earlier whispering in everyone else's ears, maybe I should step outside myself and whisper in my own ear, "Carpe Diem!"

As I watched, tears of regret and excitement filled my eyes— regret that I had missed seizing so many days, but excitement because now I felt free to experience life on my terms.

What would you do if you were invisible? When you have your answer to that question, ask yourself this question: What's preventing you from doing that now? *Carpe Diem!*

We can choose to seize each of our days by making the simple decision to move forward, which will create momentum and then confidence. The more confidence we build, the more courage develops within us to make each succeeding decision—all the while creating positive momentum in our lives to accomplish whatever goals we have.

Being aware of the momentum in our lives is important to the fulfillment we wish to achieve. The awareness of whether you are moving in a positive or negative direction will help you determine your next move. If you are in a positive state, keep doing the activities that got you there and don't stop.

REFLECTION QUESTIONS

- If you're in a negative situation right now, what's the one thing you can do to shift the momentum in a positive direction?
- Name a time in your life when you were really uncomfortable making a change or entering a new phase of your career. Once you made the change how did you feel? Did you eventually feel yourself getting comfortable with that change?
- Who do you identify most with from *The Wizard of Oz*? The lion? The tin man? The scarecrow? How so?

CHAPTER 7

PERSEVERING
THROUGH THE TOUGH TIMES

THE JOURNEY THROUGH LIFE is a story of perseverance for all of us. Whether we know it or not, at some point in our lives we have had to persevere through something. Merriam-Webster defines **perseverance** as: *continued effort to do or achieve something despite difficulties, failure, or opposition*: steadfastness.

I like to think of people who persevere as those who dig in to accomplish something, no matter what obstacles or challenges present themselves. They keep moving forward and don't quit. You may call it thick-skinned, hardnosed, determined, tenacious, or whatever you choose. The way I was raised and what I experienced as part of my family encouraged me to succeed. Nothing was going to stop me. I never once thought about succeeding at the expense of someone else, but by the sheer will and determination I had in my own heart, I persevered until I reached my goal.

Many will say life is difficult, but that depends on your perspective. Life doesn't have to be complicated, but we, as humans, make it so. One must persevere to get through life and maybe even one's job, one day at a time. It all depends on where you are on your journey. You may have been living a good life until something tragic happens. What do you do to keep moving forward? To succeed in moving forward, you must continue moving, although it is hard. If you want to get to the end of the pain or suffering, you must persevere along the journey.

The key is the awareness of the need to persevere and being aware of where you are on your journey. Know that if you do persevere, you will reap the rewards, and you will experience some sense of fulfillment when you do.

Persevering as a Family

We grew up in a household of nine—seven children and my parents plus a dog, initially in our tiny home in Northeast Baltimore. There was not much room to breathe in those conditions. In fact, my three brothers and I shared one 10x10 bedroom with double bunk beds. We were poor. Only, we really didn't know it. My mom was a stay-at-home mom, and my dad worked three jobs to make ends meet. At one point my father was laid off from his main job, leaving him with little money and several hungry children to feed.

I remember going to G.C. Murphy (a discount store) with my mom one day. I must have been about eight years old. We did our shopping, moved into the checkout line, and prepared to pay our bill. Once the cashier was finished bagging our items, she hit the total button on the cash register and gave my mom her total. My mother reached into her purse for what I thought was money. Instead she pulled out this booklet of stamps. They were food stamps, as I came to understand later. Food stamps were for people who were poor. It hit me at that moment: We were really poor; poor enough to need government assistance. (Sometimes people just need a little help, as did we, so please understand I'm not passing judgment but simply relating the thoughts of a child). I will never forget that day. In that instance something inside of me ached. I understood how my mom and dad had to persevere on a daily basis if they wanted to make it, and still we needed help. I can't imagine the stress they lived through. I decided then that I wouldn't let that happen to me when I got older.

As I mentioned earlier, my dad worked three jobs to get us through. He worked at A&P/Super Fresh for fifty-five years. In addition to his regular job, he worked part-time at the funeral parlor parking cars, and he worked as an usher at Memorial Stadium, where the Baltimore Colts once played. One benefit to the usher job was that my brother Marshall and I would get to go to the games for free. I remember packing a lunch to go to the game. My dad would buy this inexpensive package of lunchmeat. There were about ten slices in a package, and we were allowed two slices each for a sandwich—far from a club sandwich. Anyway, we would arrive at the stadium at 10 a.m. for a 2 p.m. game and sit in the first row of the center field bleachers, directly behind the end zone. As I said before, we were poor, but at the time, we really didn't know it because of some of the neat things we experienced.

A good Friday night for us would be my brother, sister, and I kneeling on the sofa, looking out the window, waiting for my dad to walk around the corner from the bus stop. He would get that good old 5-pound block of cheese from social services and take it to work with him, where he would get the cheese sliced for us. I remember how exciting it was for us to see him turn that corner.

When you don't know you're poor, the little things like getting your 5-pound block of cheese sliced from work made you feel rich.

I never heard my mom or dad complain. My mom was a devout Catholic, and my dad was an immigrant from Italy. Were they both stressed and full of anxiety? I'm sure they were, but they did their best to never show it. They persevered through many years of financial hardship to raise us the best they could. In fact, as poor as we were, my mother was hell bent on sending us to a Catholic grade school. You may be thinking, Why would you spend the money you didn't have to go to a private school when you could have saved that money by going to a public school? Although I'm sure my father argued for us to go to the public school, my mother was not going to let that happen. She is a woman of great faith and trust in God. She persevered in her faith alone.

Focused on a Goal

As a kid, I delivered newspapers in the neighborhood, at 4 a.m. and 2:30 p.m. every day. In fact, two of my brothers and sisters at that time delivered newspapers as well. That's what we had to do to make money to buy things we wanted. When winter came, I solicited as many of my newspaper customers as possible to let them know I would shovel their sidewalks when it snowed. Back then you typically got anywhere from two to five dollars to shovel a walk. On a snowy day, I would leave the house in the morning with my shovel, and my goal was to not come home until I had earned one hundred dollars for the day. No matter how cold it was or how frozen my fingers and toes were, I was not stopping until I made one hundred dollars. There were many days when I thought about quitting early because I was in so much pain, but I persisted until I hit my goal. The thing about perseverance is, if you don't have a goal or an outcome in mind, why would you continue to push? You wouldn't.

Today, people are always looking for the quick fix, the get-rich scheme, the shortest, easiest way to success. Today's society wants to go from A to Z without experiencing B through Y. If you think you were fortunate enough to go from A to Z without experiencing the journey in between, I'd say you got ripped off or sold short. The journey (or the dash) is where we learn and grow into who we're supposed to be. It's where perseverance comes into play. It's what makes persevering all the more fulfilling, by working hard and doing whatever achieving the goal requires. You may have to do something over and over again no matter how tired you are or how much pain you are in. It's like a baseball player going out on the practice field day in and day out, taking hundreds of ground balls to become a better infielder, or a dancer working on a dance routine until her body hurts so badly. When you become better at whatever you do because of the time and effort you put in, you are more fulfilled when you reach your goal. The journey is what life is all about. Perseverance molds us and develops our mantle. It's about believing in an outcome and holding true to our virtues and character to stay the course.

Paying the Price

One of my all-time favorite examples of perseverance begins with our Lord and Savior Jesus Christ. God sent us His only Son, who came to die for our sins. Christ knew His outcome before His journey began. He was mocked, tortured, and nailed to a cross, all to do the will of God. It was hard, but He knew what He had to do and why He had to do it. Christ persevered through His time here on earth to share His stories and perform His miracles so that we may come to believe and trust in Him.

You may have heard of *the Passion of Christ.* Passion comes from the word suffering. So when referencing *the Passion of Christ,* we are talking about the suffering of Christ. The suffering began as Jesus was praying in the Garden of Gethsemane while He asked His disciples to stay awake and wait for Him to finish. Christ literally sweated blood, and as you may or may not know, He was taken into custody, mocked, tortured, and crucified within a twenty-four hour period of time. Jesus had to persevere through the hardest of times to save us from our sins.

I often choose to use Christ's passion as a metaphor in my own life. If there is something I want badly, I ask myself the question, *What price am I willing to pay to obtain that which I am striving to achieve?* Think about it, a husband and wife may be going through a tough time but really want their marriage to work. They've decided that no matter how bad things are, they will commit to restoring their marriage. There will be ups and downs along the way, but they know if they persevere and are willing to suffer through the pains of any emotional wounds inflicted, they will surely live the marriage God willed for them. God wants good for us; however, He isn't giving us a free ride; we have to work for the outcome we desire. In this example, a husband and wife not only have to make a commitment to have a better marriage, they have to work at the relationship. This could mean weekly date nights, daily conversations, or listening to each other more purposefully.

They say everyone has a cross to carry. Whether it's a troubled marriage, an accident, an injury of some sort, or a special needs child you weren't ready for, God has a plan, and He never gives us more than we can handle. Someone in your family may have died an unexpected death, and now you have to persevere through the pain of that loss. Time heals, as they say, and suffering takes time to get through, but at the end of the suffering, there lays a multitude of blessings. We need to see through the pain to see the glory. When we become aware of what we need to do or the work we have to put in, we are more fulfilled when we reach our goal.

The Grind

When I think of the word "perseverance," I often relate it to the grind. Life is a *grind,* and if you want to succeed, you have to be willing to grind it out every day. Grinding it out means accepting it may not be a smooth ride. There are going to be bumps and obstacles along your journey, but if you stay the course and work through the rough spots, there will be a greater sense of appreciation and fulfillment when you achieve your goal. It's been said, "Life is a cinch by the inch but hard by the yard." If you take on projects or tasks one piece at a time or you chunk down a larger task into smaller projects, things may be easier to handle. When you look at a formidable task in front of you, the enormity of it all may cause unnecessary stress in your life. You may have children to raise, a job that requires a lot of time at work, or other responsibilities that consume most of your time. Whatever the situation, you have to manage your time appropriately to accomplish your desired goal.

BETTER THAN YOU THINK

My real estate business requires perseverance on multiple levels. Nothing is handed to you when you get into this business. You may get a few deals from those closest to you; however, no matter how well you know people, you must keep in mind you are helping someone either buying or selling their biggest asset. People don't take that lightly. The most important part about building a real estate business is generating new leads. In fact, it's the most important part of any business. Lead generation takes persistence and resilience. I commit myself to proactive tasks every day; I refer to them as "no-matter-what" activities. Numbers dictate that to be successful in real estate, you should generate leads two to three hours a day. That consists of anything from writing personal handwritten notes and making calls to stopping by clients' houses or places of work to say hello.

When lead generating, you often come up against resistance, and the biggest resistance is the so-called "drunk monkey" in your mind that tells you, *You are not good enough to do this* or makes you think *Why would anyone want to work with me?* When you hear these words in your own mind, continuing to move forward can be tough. Perseverance requires you to keep moving forward despite those fears and insecurities.

Many days when I get up in the morning, I'm not excited to write notes to people in my database or people whom I've recently met, but it's one thing I've done consistently well over the years. I recently took inventory of how many notes I have written in the seventeen years I've been in the business, and the number added up to over twenty-seven thousand notes. That's a lot of notes! Taking it a step further, that's over $10,000 in postage alone, assuming an average of 40 cents a stamp. It takes determination and perseverance to write that many notes over any period of time.

This has allowed me to achieve what has been important to me over the years, like being able to send my children to a Catholic school, having a nice home to live in, and helping those who are less fortunate than me. Determining your why when setting a goal gives you the motivation to persevere. Take some time to reflect on what's important to you and ask yourself what you are willing to do to get there.

Trials and Tribulations

Mother Teresa of Calcutta may be one of the greatest modern-day stories of a human being persevering in her faith to help others. Mother Teresa was the founder of the Order of the Missionaries, which was a Roman Catholic congregation of women dedicated to helping the poor. Her story is one of compassion and perseverance. At the age of eighteen she decided to become a nun. For seventeen years she dedicated herself to being a teacher until she felt another calling. She was called by God to abandon her teaching and go to the slums of Calcutta to help the city's sickest and poorest people.

Through her efforts she was able to impact millions of people around the world. Over a long period of time, as her ministry grew, she was able to attract donations locally and worldwide. She didn't set out to be a celebrity or attract attention for the wrong reasons. To do what she did demanded a high level of dedication and perseverance. She helped the poorest of the poor, the sick and diseased, the homeless, and more. She lived in an undesirable environment where food and water were scarce. There was always going to be another sick person or another homeless person. Her mission was never-ending. Few people would ever be able to endure what Mother Teresa endured. Schools were opened for children, and she established housing for the dying, leper colonies, orphanages, a nursing home, a family clinic, and a number of other health clinics.

Mother Teresa died in September of 1997 after dedicating fifty years to her work. Fifty years! In October of 2003 she was named a saint in a ceremony led by Pope John Paul II. Her dedication and accomplishments are the modern-day definition of perseverance.

What's somewhat troubling and inspiring about her story is that in private correspondence revealed after her death, she had discussed her faith. She felt she was alone for most of those fifty years of her work. She was living in darkness. She felt God was nowhere to be seen. She even made reference to not wanting to utter the words she felt and the pain of the loneliness she experienced. Not only did she have to persevere through the physical conditions of her environment and the people she helped, but Mother Teresa also had to persevere through her own mental darkness. It took courage for her to persevere when she could have given up at any time. But through all of this she remained steadfast in her work.

What's important to note here is this: Despite her saintliness, Mother Teresa was able to relate to other human beings, and people are still able to make a connection with her. Millions and millions of people living today are experiencing loneliness and doubt. They may ask, *Where is God in all this?* To know Mother Teresa's story is to know perseverance. In believing she was doing what she was called to do, she not only helped the millions of people during her lifetime, but she is still impacting lives today.

REFLECTION QUESTIONS

- Reflect on your own life and think of some of the tough times you have been through.
- What were some of your darkest moments?
- When did you feel lonely?
- How did you persevere through these times?
- What gave you the courage to persevere?

Prayer

Prayer also involves perseverance. In a society that wants things yesterday, it's tough to continually ask God for His blessings day after day when you don't see the answers immediately or you never see them at all. God wants us to continually come to Him. In not answering our prayers, sometimes He is answering them.

One evening my daughter and I were driving along in the car, talking about the Bible. I asked her if she felt she had a good relationship with Jesus. She said, "I think I do, but I wonder if He gets mad at me for asking for the same thing over and over." (What a brilliant statement for a fourteen-year-old to make!)

I responded, "That was so awesome to hear you say that! God will never get angry with you for asking for something over and over again. He wants us to continually come to Him and ask. For you to keep asking for something of God shows that you have faith in Him and you believe if you continue to ask, He will answer your prayers. He loves it when we are persistent with Him." When we pray, we should never expect an immediate response. We must persevere in our prayer for a lifetime. The answers we get are not always the answers we want, but we will always get answers. The answers are God's answers, not ours.

Contemplative prayer is a form of prayer requiring one to have discipline, and it requires a massive amount of perseverance. You must quiet your mind despite all of the thoughts you experience. Have you ever attempted to quiet your mind of all your thoughts? It's an unbelievably difficult task. You have fifty thousand thoughts running through your mind a day, and all of the sudden, for a period of time you want your mind to shut down? It's tough! To reach a contemplative state, you must center yourself first by thinking a sacred word or phrase, not more than a few syllables, and then repeat it every time a thought crosses your mind. You will fight thought after thought until eventually your mind is quiet. But to recognize silence is a thought as well.

There can be days and days where you attempt to contemplate and the barrage of thoughts consuming you will not stop. You think you are failing, but you're not. You are actually working out that muscle of prayer, and then one day it all comes together. It takes quite a bit of perseverance to get to a place of silence, but in time it can happen. You may be sitting to pray when you will experience interior and exterior distractions. You may hear a noise or experience one of those irritating itches you just need to scratch. You must ignore those things and do nothing. It takes discipline and perseverance to ignore the distractions, but once you create the momentum, you must continue to move forward in your prayer, and in time you will begin to notice a change.

Persevering as a Parent

In parenting, perseverance plays a huge role. I have been a dad for a long time now, and in my opinion, being a parent is the greatest gift in the world as well as a huge challenge. I think any parent would agree that teaching and coaching your children can push you to your limits. As a child, there was a time when I thought I knew more than my parents, and I guess it's payback time now. My mother used to tell me how stubborn I was as a child and how I fought her on everything. I constantly challenge my children to be the best they can be, and boy, do they push back, doing the exact opposite.

My son, Robbie, is a naturally gifted athlete. You won't see him in the NBA or Major League Baseball, but he is an above-average athlete. One thing I didn't pick up on early was his anxiety over playing on a team. I figured it was something every kid went through, and he would eventually grow out of it. That wasn't the case.

Robbie started playing basketball at school. He wasn't a starter. In fact, he wasn't getting much playing time at all. We were about five games into his fifth-grade season when he got injured. He was going to be out for three to four weeks. I told him all he could do while he was hurt was to practice dribbling and taking foul shots.

I came home from work one day, pulled into the driveway, and hit my garage door button in the car. As the door rose, I saw this little body and a ball bouncing. As the door went a little higher, there was Robbie dribbling a basketball—blindfolded. He was dribbling with both hands, through his legs, and at one point, was dribbling two balls at the same time. My heart melted because not only had he taken the advice, but he was also able to make himself a better player while being hurt. Once he returned from the injury, it wasn't long before he became a starter.

Two things happened here: One, we had to persevere as parents to coach him through his injury, and two, Robbie was able to persevere during his downtime and become a better ball player, not to mention a starter.

As a parent you push and push; you encourage and stay as positive as you can, and you never give up. You don't always get your children to do what you think is best, but you keep trying and never stop the encouragement. Perseverance is a requirement for all parents. Not only did we need to encourage and coach him in sports, but we also had to coach him through his anxieties in life. Most parents go through this to some degree, some more than others, but we must continue to stay the course and persevere through the tough moments for the benefit of our children.

Years ago, my family went on a vacation to our home in Deep Creek Lake in western Maryland. It was our first trip to the house during the winter season. Our plan was to do some snow tubing and skiing. I had only been skiing a half dozen times or so; Debbie, my wife, once; and Robbie and Amanda, never.

During beginner ski lessons, they teach the basics of how to speed up and slow down. To speed up, you keep your skis parallel to each other pointing straight ahead. This is referred to as French fries. If you're moving downhill and want to slow down, you form a triangle from the tip of your skis, going out on an angle to the back of your skis. This is referred to as the pizza. So the basic concept for beginners was always French fries, pizza, French fries, pizza.

It started out rough for all three of them. After several falls and many frustrations, they were beginning to get the hang of it. Robbie picked it up a little quicker, but still struggled. The lesson finally ended, and Robbie and Amanda couldn't have been happier. There was one more task in front of us.

Happy to have finished the lesson, we headed to the ski lodge to grab lunch. On the way to the lodge, I stopped Robbie and Amanda to tell them the instructor had given me one more piece of instruction for them before the lesson would officially be considered finished. I told them that after they finished lunch, they both had to ski down the beginner hill by themselves without poles and without falling. Of course, none of that was true, but I wanted to see how far I could push them. They weren't real happy with me at that moment, but I convinced them that was the instruction I had been given.

Soon after, we were heading back in the direction of the beginner hill. Both Robbie and Amanda went to the top of the hill while Debbie and I watched from below. Robbie went first and with no issues made it to the bottom. His lesson was complete.

Amanda was struggling. Time and again she attempted to make it down the hill without falling, but she failed each time. Amanda looked as though she had had enough. So Robbie and I went off to ski a few other trails. We would check in with Debbie and Amanda in a bit.

An hour or so later, we were back, and Amanda and Debbie were not having fun. We talked about giving it another try. I continued to coach Amanda, "French fries, pizza, French fries, pizza," I yelled. She continued to struggle and fall. As she lay on the ground, face down, after her last fall, I told her I was ready to leave. My impatience with her inability to get down the hill just once was at its limit. When I told her to get up because we were leaving, she turned and looked at me with a tear streaming down her cheek and said, "No, I'm not quitting!" I was shocked at her response yet pleasantly surprised. *My daughter was not going to quit.* I was so proud of her. I responded, "One last try! If you make it all the way down the hill without falling, we will stay. If you don't, we are leaving."

Amanda rose to her feet and took the conveyer belt to the top of her hill. Before she left, I whispered in her ears, "French fries, pizza, French fries, pizza." She got to the top and was ready to go. Slowly she skied down the hill, from side to side. She started out wobbly but soon regained her balance. A third of the way down, she was looking strong. "French fries, pizza!" I was yelling. She was halfway down, and I believed she could make it. Her confidence was growing, and she began to move faster down the hill. As she neared the bottom, my eyes welled up with tears. *She's going to make it,* I thought. A few more yards and she made it! Now we could celebrate! I gave her a high five and a great big hug. I couldn't have been more proud of her. She was not going to quit, and to this day she still has that same toughness about her.

REFLECTION QUESTIONS

- **Think back on moments in your life when you had to persevere as a parent. Did you maintain your patience?**
- **How did you persevere when you felt like giving up?**
- **Were you aware of what you needed to do as a parent to encourage your child to persevere?**
- **Did you find fulfillment in the moment your child succeeded?**

Believe in What You're Doing and Why

To persevere is to believe in an outcome—or your purpose—despite what lies in front of you. Mother Teresa believed in what she was doing. Despite her darkness and loneliness, she continued to move forward with her purpose to help the sick and destitute. Jesus Christ continued the work of His Father in the midst of all the criticism and charges brought against Him. He came into this world to save us from our sins and was nailed to a cross. He knew His purpose and the outcome, yet He persevered until His death. He still perseveres to this day as He continues to knock on the door of our hearts, asking each of us individually to allow Him into our lives.

My daughter persevered in her desire to learn how to ski. I persevered to get up each morning at an early hour to earn money to pay my way through high school and college. There are millions and millions of people out there who persist in their calling every day to serve a purpose. Millions of people have to do so each day, week, month, and year in their work. Although it may not be their calling, they do it to survive or to provide for others. I'm always reminded of the thought that my dad worked fifty-five years for one company. Fifty-five years! That's amazing and a great example of perseverance. When we persevere no matter how hard the effort may be, or how impossible the goal may seem, the rewards are tremendous. The biggest reward of all is the fulfillment we receive in our hearts and our minds when we embrace the journey and accomplish our goal.

Where in Your Life Have You Had to Persevere?

Reflect for a time and think back in all areas of your life where you had to persevere through something. Create a story file of your experiences and revisit them periodically so that you may appreciate all that you have been through. Perseverance builds character and makes us better. When we embrace these moments and accept them as they are, the world opens up to us and blessings lay right around the corner.

For me, I like to go through these areas in my life: spiritual, family, business, financial, and personal. I reflect on my journey and appreciate all that has happened and how it has led to me becoming who I am. It also has prepared me for future challenges that I now see as opportunities. (As a place to journal your thoughts on perseverance you can grab the free companion workbook at robcommodariauthor.com/workbook.)

To persevere is to never give up and to never give in!

CHAPTER 8

KNOWING YOUR HEART'S DESIRES

WE HAVE ALL SEEN those crazy Capital One credit card commercials that end with the question, "What's in your wallet?" Well, I would like to begin this chapter with this question: What's in your heart?

I ask that for a number of reasons. At the time of this writing, I finished watching an episode of *American Idol*. What I love most about the show is how many contestants get up on stage to audition who really believe in their ability to sing. For those really trying to succeed, it's the heart of the contestants and their stories that resonate with me. I love when someone gets on stage and immediately connects with the panel. Many times a contestant will walk on stage with a look that makes you question what the heck they are doing there. Then, surprisingly, this unbelievable voice comes out. It's not only coming out of their mouth; it's coming from their heart.

You know a connection is made with the panel when you see the judges get teary eyed or they start moving and shaking.

Their eyes may open wide, and they may make a comment about having goose bumps in that moment. The point is, it's obvious there is a connection.

There are many definitions of heart, and for purposes of this chapter, I am choosing to use the definition from Merriam-Webster: *one having courage or enthusiasm especially when maintained during a difficult situation and to see one's innermost character, feelings, or inclinations.*

So, I ask you, what's in your heart? I have known since July 1990 when I read my first personal growth and self-help book, *The Greatest Salesman in the World,* that I wanted to write and share with the world what is in my heart. I'm a kid from the city who has always wanted to make an impact. It was difficult growing up, as you have read earlier, and I do realize many people have had it worse. However, I believe my purpose is to inspire people to believe in their dreams and to realize those dreams through perseverance and passionate activity. I want to help you become aware of what inspires you to fulfill your goals.

My Love for Baseball

When I was five years old, I knew I wanted to be a professional baseball player. Yes, I know a lot of young boys feel that way. But I knew it in my heart. I can remember wanting to play organized baseball as a six-year-old, only I wasn't allowed to because I wasn't old enough. Leagues back then started at eight years of age. I was six, and I had this feeling in my heart I was as good as the boys who were eight. It's like that tuning fork that hums in your heart when you feel really good about something. When you feel it, you have to act on it, especially if it points you in the direction of your goals.

When you know something in your heart, you feel it. It's an instinct. It's a feeling of enthusiasm that wants to release itself from your body and let the world know what it is you're all about. I did things as an eight-year-old that no one had to tell me to do. I remember taking money from my allowance and purchasing Johnny Bench Batter Up (a gadget to help people become better hitters). No one encouraged me to do it. I saw the infomercial on television and I knew I wanted to be a good hitter. I bought it, set it up on my own, and practiced hitting the baseball every day. I practiced hitting right-handed and left-handed. I was a little guy, and I instinctively knew I had to work harder to get better. I remember taking an Indian Rubber baseball and working on my throwing every other day for fifteen minutes at a time. By the time I was a senior in high school and on to college, I had a pretty good arm. I could hit, run, and throw. Again, no one told me to do these things; I knew in my heart that if I wanted to do better, I had to be better. I knew what I wanted, and no one or nothing was going to stop me. I wound up being a pretty good hitter in my high school and junior college career. Heck, in my sophomore season of junior college, I was 5'8", weighed 155 pounds soaking wet, and could hit the crap out of a baseball. Back then, I hit twelve home runs in a thirty-five-game season.

The year before that (as a freshman at the Community College of Baltimore County), I had earned the starting center field job, but it didn't work out well for me. Our season opened up in Florida with six games. I didn't fare too well on the trip. Upon arriving home, I was benched. Coach Elliott Oppenheim, for whom I am forever grateful, played a guy by the name of Theron Todd in my place in center field. Theron went on to hit twenty plus homeruns, became an All American, and was drafted by the Atlanta Braves and played for the Durham Bulls, their farm team. There wasn't much I could say about it. I had my opportunity, but I just didn't play well enough to keep my spot. I hated riding the bench. For me, a guy who had started and starred at every level up to that point, this was extremely hard to handle. I was determined not to let this ever happen again. Jim Rohn, an inspirational writer and speaker, once said, "Don't wish it were easier, wish you were better." I was going to do whatever it took to start the next season and not relinquish my spot. I knew I was better than I had performed.

During the summer I worked out every day, both with weights and with baseball drills. When the next season began, during a casual conversation with my coach, he basically told me he thought I was going to be his best player that year. I swear I must have looked at him in total shock. This guy had benched me for an entire year, and now he was telling me I would be his best player. I did not take this opportunity for granted. I was the MVP of the team that year! My point here is not to brag. It's to say that no matter how bad things seem or get, if you have heart and you persevere by digging deep and working hard, there is almost nothing that can stop you.

In 1987, I received a partial scholarship to play baseball at Florida Atlantic University (FAU). A kid from Northeast Baltimore, weighing in at 155 pounds, was going to play big-time baseball in South Florida. *I'm on my way to the big leagues*, I thought. Well, it didn't quite work out that way, but boy did I learn a lot.

The fall season went well, and then the regular season began. My first official at bat at FAU was actually a home run. But nine games into the season, I suffered a stress fracture in my right foot. Fortunately, I hadn't played ten games. If I had, I would have used up a complete year of athletic eligibility. Instead, I was given a medical hardship and received an additional year of eligibility to complete my athletic college career. During the time I was injured, I didn't feel sorry for myself. Instead, I took advantage of the downtime to work out in the gym and learn the game of baseball at a strategic level. In fact, I would sit next to the head coach, Kevin Cooney, every game. It was time to listen and learn the game of baseball.

I learned so much from Coach Cooney. He was a New Jersey guy, and with me being a kid from Baltimore City, we kind of had this Northeast/Mid Atlantic kindred spirit going on. We would talk the entire game about baseball and about life. That year on the disabled list gave me the opportunity to learn something new, and for that I am deeply grateful.

The next season came and went without much fanfare. I started and played okay. I was an average hitter that year and didn't really do much. Then came my final year of school and baseball. It started off pretty well. I was healthy and hitting the ball hard during training before the season started. This was going to be my year! Not so fast. About ten to fifteen games into the season, I began to feel a familiar pain in my foot. Only this time it was in my left foot, but in the exact same spot as the stress fracture I had suffered two years earlier in my right foot. I could only hope and pray my senior year wasn't going to end with another trip to the disabled list.

We were playing Purdue one evening at our home field in Boca Raton, and I was in center field. Purdue had a runner on second base, and the batter hit a base hit up the middle right at me. As I fielded the ball and planted my left foot to make a throw to the plate, something gave way in my foot and I threw the ball into the ground about four feet in front of me, as I fell to the ground in pain. I knew immediately what it was—another stress fracture and the end of my college baseball career. All I had ever wanted to do as a kid was play baseball, and this was how it was going to end. I was devastated!

After getting the X-rays back and talking to the doctor, I was told I might heal in time to play the last couple weeks of the year. I wore a cast for two weeks to keep my foot isolated in hopes of it healing faster. Sure enough, with about two weeks to go before the end of my college baseball career, I was cleared to play.

Although I was an outfielder, two of my favorite players of all time up until then were Brooks Robinson of the Baltimore Orioles and Rico Petrocelli of the Boston Red Sox. Both players were third basemen and extremely good at their positions. We were playing the last game of the season and of my career against the University of Tampa in Tampa, Florida. Coach Cooney approached me prior to the game and told me this was my day. He said I could play any position I wanted to for my last game, and without hesitation, I chose to play third base. It may have been the most fun and most relaxed I had ever felt playing baseball in my entire career. I had six plays that day with no errors. Baseball was what I loved and all I had ever wanted to do from the time I was five years old, and now it was over.

I share this story for a reason. Just a few weeks prior, a sports banquet was held at FAU to recognize all the athletes' accomplishments throughout the year. When it was time to announce the baseball awards, Coach Cooney approached the podium. When he announced the Unsung Hero award, he said, "When my son grows up, I want him to be just like this young man on our team. Our Unsung Hero award goes to Rob Commodari." I was surprised and humbled at the same time. Coach went on to explain what I went through in two of my three years there and described me as having a lot of heart. It was an emotional moment for me and an extremely memorable one at that. I am grateful for the relationship I built with Coach Cooney and everything he taught me about baseball and life.

My three years on the team—from a baseball perspective—were not exactly what I had dreamed; however, I was able to experience life. I left my Northeast Baltimore home at the age of twenty and went to school in one of the richest counties in the country. FAU was eleven hundred miles from home, and I didn't know a soul. I was going to a new state to experience a new culture, to meet a whole new set of friends, and to experience life. My dream was to play baseball, and even though it didn't work out from a professional standpoint, I know I followed my heart and I am so proud of what I was able to experience.

Do these stories resonate with you? Being benched inspired me to be better. Although I did get down on myself initially, I used this experience to motivate me to be a better ball player. This is an experience you can use in life and work as well. For me, if I fail to get a listing in my business, I will ask the seller what I could have done differently to earn the business. If I make a mistake at home or with my family, I reflect on it and ask myself what I could have done better so as not to have made the mistake.

REFLECTION QUESTIONS

- **Think about moments of so-called failure and how you responded. Did your response come from the heart?**
- **Did your response make you a better person or did it make you better in your business?**

Bruce

Growing up, I was never much of a Bruce Springsteen fan. I knew a few songs, "Born in the USA," "Glory Days," and others. When tickets went on sale for his concert at the Baltimore arena, my wife and I decided to go. As the concert date approached, I didn't experience much of an internal buildup of excitement. My intention was to go to the show with my wife and enjoy a night out. On our way to the concert, my wife and I looked at each other questioning why we were even going to the event, as neither one of us knew many of his songs. I suggested, with a smile, that we just enjoy the expensive date and the show.

At approximately 8:00 p.m., Bruce Springsteen and the E-Street Band walked on stage and the crowd went nuts. It was an older crowd, but there was a fair share of young people there as well. Bruce opened with "The Ties That Bind" (I had never heard that song before) and went on to play for three and a half hours straight. There was no intermission nor breaks of any kind, just one song after another. Bruce told stories leading into the songs. He owned the stage! There was a ramp that extended out from the stage and then across the floor to the other side of the venue and back onto the stage. Bruce walked across this extension several times throughout the evening. He body-surfed and engaged the crowd. He even took a few selfies along the way as he stopped and shook hands with people. It was an amazing scene!

I stood and watched and took it all in. Bruce would start a song, and then the crowd would take over and sing along with him. There wasn't a fancy light show of any kind. No lasers or high-tech gimmicks; just Bruce being Bruce. The crowd was into every song, and the energy was amazing. I ran into a client of mine prior to the start of the concert and told him I had never seen Bruce Springsteen before and I didn't know many of his songs. He told me not to worry, by the end of the night I would be transformed. To my surprise, the first words Bruce spoke when he grabbed the microphone were, "Are you ready to be transformed?"

I knew what he meant about being transformed. It was about being transformed into a Bruce Springsteen fan, and that certainly became a fact three and a half hours later. But something else was happening internally as I heard those words. I thought about all the personal growth seminars I had attended over the years. I thought about the books I had read and the CDs and tapes I had listened to. I thought about what being transformed really meant to me.

In today's society most people conform to what society wants or expects of them. Very few people allow a transformation to take place. Conformity begins on the outside and works its way in. By contrast, transformation begins on the inside and works its way out.

When transformation takes place, we are allowing what is really in our hearts to come to the surface. We are transformed into who we were meant to be. That's a huge order, because the best research on personal growth and development suggests that only 3 percent of society is willing to take the journey of transformation.

Bruce Springsteen has been playing music for over forty years. I don't think at this point in his career, he does it for the money. He is playing because that's what he loves to do. Yes, he is an entertainer and his profession requires him to perform, but his energy is off the charts. With a little amazement and a lot of respect, I realized at some point during the concert that I was watching a 66-year-old guy bringing it with all he had. He wears his heart on his sleeve and the effect he has on a crowd is immeasurable! The inspiration of his lyrics and the energy he shares are impactful beyond measure. Bruce is living his passion and his purpose.

One of my favorite Springsteen songs is "Rising." Not only does the beat of the song resonate with me, but the lyrics speak to my heart. I'm a guy who expects so much of myself, and when I fall short, I can be hard on myself without taking time to reflect on where I have been and how far I have come.

I have come a long way in my life and still have so much more to accomplish, but I wouldn't be here without following the desires of my heart. It's not all smooth sailing, as you can imagine. There are days when I can see the fruits of my labor and there are many more when I feel like I can't see any progress. That's why it's so important to not only track or journal your progress (get this book's companion workbook for free at robcommodariauthor. com/workbook), but to reflect on it and be aware of the progress you're making. It's during the quiet time when things come to light, but if you have too much going on or too much noise in your head, there is no way to feel the progress.

I continued to think and dwell in the moment as I watched and listened to Bruce. I had thoughts of sadness and thoughts of excitement. My sadness came from a point of questioning whether I was living my purpose and whether or not it was too late to be who I wanted to be or was created to be. Had I let too much time pass by? I knew better then to fall into the trap of self-pity and guilt. So, I switched gears and my negative thoughts, and decided to think of what's still to come and how I could be an inspiration to people going forward.

I have to encourage people every day in my real estate career. It's a great feeling to help people realize their dreams of home ownership. Not only do I get to help people realize those dreams, but I also have the opportunity to influence and inspire other agents in this business. I built a successful real estate career from the ground up. I want something bigger though; bigger than buying and selling real estate. I want to help people fulfill their potential as I achieve mine.

My goal or dream has been to impact and inspire people to believe in their dreams and to realize those dreams through perseverance and passionate activity. I do this through my speaking and writing. My only hope is that when I am 66 years old, I am still bringing it and still living with that same energy and purpose that I saw Bruce Springsteen show on stage!

REFLECTION QUESTIONS

- **What energy are you putting out there?**
- **Are you giving it your all? If not, what's preventing you from doing so?**
- **Where in your life can you give a little more effort?**

Speak from the Heart

A close friend of mine, Mark Brodinsky, once wrote, "When you speak from the heart, everyone who has one will buy in." So often in life when we speak, we want people to listen. But so many people speak from their rear end all day long. They are either selling you a load of crap or they want to be recognized so badly that they embellish everything in every way they can, just to receive a hollow acknowledgement. But when you speak from the heart, you capture the attention of your audience and you become attractive. People will hang on your every word.

You may have heard people say you shouldn't wear your heart on your sleeve. I understand some people can go overboard, but whenever I speak to people, I want them to know it's coming from my heart, so that's what I give them. If you trust in who you are and mean well, others are going to feel your energy. They will feel you speaking from your heart.

There was a time years ago when I was in a real estate coaching program, and a buddy of mine, Rob Foy, and I had decided to start a regional group of real estate agents who would get together once a quarter to mastermind. It was set up so that each one of us would give a presentation, and then we would have these breakout sessions to further discuss the topic presented. I loved the idea of presenting on stage: I dreamed about writing a best-selling book and being on stage speaking to millions of people. I was going to be rich! I was going to be famous!

One day I was on this small stage presenting to about a hundred real estate agents. While I was giving my presentation, I hoped to be impressive, and I looked forward to receiving lots of compliments later. Remember, at this time I was all about me and how good I could look on stage, but something struck me right in the middle of the presentation. Call it God, my conscience, my guardian angel, whatever it was, but it spoke to me: *Who do you think you are? This is not about you. This is about others!* Right in that moment I had a change of heart. It's hard to explain except to say nothing changed at all with the material I was presenting. All that changed was the mindset I had as to why I was presenting. Not for me, but for them.

Another buddy of mine, Paul Hunter, was recording the presentation. When we were finished, he approached me and said, "Rob, that was the best presentation I've seen you give!" I knew in that instant *why*; because I had experienced a change of heart right there in the middle of a presentation on a stage in front of those hundred or so agents to make it about them and not about me. When you speak from the heart, people buy in, and when you speak for the benefit of others, people feel connected. It was an amazing feeling to have that change of heart.

Recently, I had a conversation with a friend of mine. We get together every month or two and talk about life, work, and spirituality. Our conversations always go deep. One of his consistent comments over the years has been that he always feels my energy when we get together. He says he feels it when I talk to him; he knows the words and thoughts are coming from my heart. People know when you're not being honest with them, and they know when you are being authentic. Authenticity and transparency are attractive; inauthenticity pushes people away and gives them pause about whether or not they can trust you. Speak from the heart and people buy in.

REFLECTION QUESTIONS

- **Are you speaking from the heart?**
- **Are you making this life about yourself or others?**
- **Reflect for a moment and decide what needs to change, if anything, in how you show up in every conversation to be more authentic.**

Play with Heart

Whether it's sports or another activity, when you give it all you've got and play with all your heart, good things happen. Do you play from your heart? Growing up, I played sports with friends of mine almost every day. One friend had tons of talent. He was gifted with natural ability, and most people thought he was going to make it in professional sports. But he didn't give it all he had. I would say he "pulled a heart muscle." He was gifted, and I guess he took it for granted, and things just didn't work out for him. Failing does not necessarily mean you have no heart, but not having heart is a good way to ensure you fail.

I live and play the game of life with all my heart. God has blessed me with so much, and when I look back at my life and think of all the blessings He has bestowed on me and my family, I believe it's because I gave Him my heart and I gave it all I had to be the best I could be. I bring an intensity to all I do, and it can be overwhelming to some people at times. I have to remind myself when to pull back and when to push forward.

It's obvious what happens when you play this game of life from your heart. From the *American Idol* contestants and Bruce Springsteen to the average person who lives life authentically, good things happen when you give it all you've got. We're not all going to be movie stars, professional musicians, actors, or athletes. However, no matter what your calling in life is, if you live from the heart, you will be fulfilled and blessed in ways you can't imagine.

CHAPTER 9

FINDING YOUR PASSION

WHAT ARE YOU passionate about? We are often asked this question, and most people do not have an answer. To help you find your passion, first let's look at the definition and root of the word. From Merriam-Webster, **passion:** *a strong feeling or emotion.* A secondary definition is *an object of someone's love, liking, or desire. It can also mean to have excitement or enthusiasm about something; any powerful or compelling emotion or feeling, as love or hate.*

The origin of the word passion comes from the word "suffering." When Christians hear the word passion, they often think of the Passion of Christ. How Christ suffered and died for us. Let's go back to the original question: What are you passionate about? Sometimes people don't truly understand the context of the question, so I'll phrase it another way. If you didn't need money or have to worry about getting paid, what would you do in your life?

Thinking about what you're passionate about leads to the next question. What would you be willing to die for? Again, Jesus

Christ suffered and died for us. He was passionate about that. When you think about your career, your family, or something you really want to do in your life, are you willing to suffer for it? Would you metaphorically be willing to die for it?

Finding My First Passion

After graduating from college, I took a job at a stock brokerage firm in North Palm Beach, Florida. I didn't know what I was getting myself into at the time. All I wanted to do was make as much money as I could and repay my parents for all they had done for me throughout the years. I took a job at a penny stock firm. It was a great learning experience. It was a young, energetic office of go-getters. Everyone was extremely welcoming and willing to help everyone else succeed at a high level.

One guy by the name of Valentino Fernandez took me under his wing almost immediately. We sat next to each other in our cubicles. He had been there just over a year when I first started, and he was doing very well. Valentino had come to America from Cuba and was passionate about succeeding. On the weekends, he would take me out on his boat and we would go boarding or tubing. All the while he was giving me tips on how to be successful in this business. Every day I would pepper him with questions. He never wavered to answer, and he was always there to help.

One morning I arrived early at the office to see a book lying on Valentino's desk. Later that day, I asked him about it, and he lent it to me. The book was called *The Greatest Salesman in the World*. It was written by Og Mandino, and it launched my passion for reading books and discovering my purpose. After that first night reading it, I had this humming in my heart and I felt a strong calling to pursue this path of personal growth to be the best I could be in order to help others be their best. I decided that I was going to learn all I could about becoming an example for others and invigorating everyone I came into contact with with insights about living their dreams.

In order to be able to speak from an exemplary position, I had to educate myself about what it meant to be inspirational and invigorating. Was it something innate? Was it a mindset that you can turn on and off? Did it require a particular life experience?

In the beginning, I just wanted to learn *how* to do it. How could I become the person people would want to seek out for insights about their own beating hearts? I felt that if I was this guy who came from modest means and figured out how to live life to the fullest, people would want to hear about it. People would want to know how leaning into my passion allowed me to lead a fulfilling life and whether they could discover the same; how fulfilling a life they could have.

For the next several years, I read hundreds of books on the topics of self-help and personal growth, looking for the trigger that would turn on my inspirational qualities. Even after I switched jobs and started a business in the newspaper industry, I made sure to arrive early at the newspaper distribution center and crack open a book. I didn't let a day go by in which I didn't have a book with me. At the end of the day, even an extremely busy one that had totally wiped me out, I would make sure to read at least one page before going to sleep.

Awareness of the Calling

When I meet with people and we get into a discussion about life and its multiple meanings, I'm instantly aware of the energy in my body rising to another level. The energy I get is a clue for me to consider this journey of personal growth and development as my calling, particularly from a speaking and writing standpoint. I feel fulfilled when helping people discover ways to expand themselves. And if you asked me whether I would do this work without getting paid to do it, the answer would be an unequivocal YES!

If you're not sure of what your purpose or calling is, you need to look or listen for clues. As I mentioned in the previous paragraph, pay attention to your energy level when you talk about a particular subject or when you listen to the words of a song and they resonate with you at a deep level. It could be a book you're reading or a movie you're watching. Clues show up when you least expect it. There may be something there for you. Being aware of that energy is the beginning, then taking action is the next step.

Now, obviously, I still need to pay my bills and buy food to eat and raise our kids and donate to those who need financial help. Since I still need to cover my expenses, I am most certainly happy to talk to audiences for a fee! But if I had all the money in the world, or at least if money were not a need or an issue, I would certainly talk in front of audiences for free! And that to me is certainly a sign of a true passion.

We all have a calling or a purpose. My calling is to help people discover what their purpose is. I am fulfilled when I can lift people up to show them how unique and special they are. And the methods I most enjoy employing to help people rise up are speaking and writing. That is my true passion, and that's where I experience the greatest fulfillment.

If you follow your passion in life, there is no doubt you will impact people in some way. God put us all on this earth for a purpose, yet He gives us free will to choose our own paths. He wants us to experience life's lessons for ourselves and discover the person we can be along the way. The lessons we learn make us who we are, and what makes each of us distinctly ourselves is where we find the kernel of value that we can bring to others. But we can only make that journey of discovery if we are willing to search for and recognize our passion. If we don't pursue our passion, I doubt at the end of our short stay on this beautiful earth we will feel fulfilled with the life we have lived.

Mr. Personal Growth

So, I kept reading and searching for lessons that inspired me. I had created a new awareness about myself and about life, and I was certain that what inspired me surely was inspiring to everyone else.

I believed I had the answer to everyone's problems. Everywhere I went I would talk to people—friends, family members, work associates, even strangers and acquaintances—about personal growth. I tried to force my passion on others because I believed if it was good for me, then everyone else needed it as well. I would give books to friends, and a week later I would ask if they had read it yet. I soon learned that not many people were drawn to reading as much as I was. It came to a point where I felt people were shying away from me.

I realize now where I may have been over the top with my

enthusiasm (let's just call it zealotry), but I was only doing so because I wanted to help others share the same valuable epiphanies that I had.

I still read every day, but I've learned over the years that I don't have to club people over the head with my passion. Instead, I wait and allow myself to be invited in. Instead of suffocating people with information about personal growth, I pause to let them feel my peace and to ask how I came to my center. That's my invitation! It's also the only way to be truly helpful. I can't just yell at people, "Look at how much I've read. I've got oodles of inspiration in me!"

Once people begin to reveal to me what they think, once they start inquiring about my attitude toward a particular subject, then I can ask the questions that uncover where they are in their lives and learn which direction they want to go. At that point, I can offer some perspective about what hinders or holds them back from doing the things that matter most to them. Then I can share with them what I've learned along the way, and I can make suggestions for reading or audio books that fit into their outlook and can open them up to seeing things through a different lens.

Discovering What Impassions Others

My learned patience in discovering what motivates people rather than assuming they are inspired by the same things I am has had its rewards. In the summer before my son Robbie started college, we decided this was the year we were going to go skydiving in Ocean City, Maryland.

If you've not tried it, skydiving is transcendental. It is completely breathtaking, literally, but it is also hyper-stimulating.

Your physical senses are on overload, yet you feel like you exist entirely on a spiritual plane.

When Robbie and I reached the earth after dropping ten thousand feet, we looked at one another but didn't say a word. I had the sense that if either of us tried to say anything, we would both get choked up. We just shared a bear hug. As we were driving back to the condo, I asked Robbie what he thought of the jump. All he could say was, "Dad, I'm speechless." I could only respond with, "Me too."

Over the next few months, several people asked Robbie about his skydiving experience, and he responded that it was hard to explain. Then, he went off to college. Several weeks later, he called me and told me he was reading *Training Camp* by Jon Gordon, a book that I had given him. He asked me if I would read page 152 of the book when I had a chance. It's the part where an athlete named Martin, a free-agent rookie, is trying out for a team. During his first exhibition game, he twists his ankle and is injured for a couple weeks. He is stressed out because he needs the position to make the money to pay for his mom's heart transplant. Long story short, he gets involved with an assistant coach who takes him under his wing and teaches him about what matters in life. Eventually, Martin's injury heals, and he does great at his last tryout. He makes the team and heads over to the assistant coach's office to celebrate with him only to find that the coach had had a heart attack and died the night before. Stunned, Martin goes to the beach and reflects on all that the coach taught him during their short time together. He dives into a wave and comes up with his hands in the air, feeling exhilarated by all he has learned from his mentor.

Robbie says to me, "Dad, that's what it felt like to jump out of that plane."

I was thrilled that a book allowed my son to have the breakthrough to be able to articulate what makes him feel *alive*. But here's where the circle comes full: Just as it took me hundreds of books and years of discovery to know what impassioned me, it has taken the same amount of time to figure out that others are moved by many different passions. We are connected by all the things that make us unique. The universality of our ability to feel passionately and to be able to share it with others is what makes us feel whole.

REFLECTION QUESTIONS

- **Are you aware of your calling? If so, what is it?**
- **Are you aware of what impassions those closest to you? If so, who are those people and how do you know what impassions them?**
- **Can you recall the first time you got excited about a job, a person, or a hobby? What did you feel?**

Learning from my Parents

I saw my parents do what they needed to do to raise us the way they did. They were passionate about the way they raised us. They suffered through some tough times as they struggled financially, and my parents were willing to put aside any self-interests to see us do well. My parents raised seven of us and did a pretty good job, I would say. But it wasn't without challenges. My mom was determined for all of us to get a Catholic education, no matter what. My Italian immigrant father worked three jobs to help support the family and send us to a Catholic primary school. I never knew anyone who worked as hard as my dad, and never once did I hear him complain.

My father passed onto me the good work ethic I currently enjoy. There was never a question about whether I would be a diligent worker. I worked from childhood. I literally started working at 11 years old, and I worked all the way through high school and college. When I was ready to start high school, my parents said to me, you can go to the public high school for free or you can pay to go to the Catholic high school, but we can't afford to help so you'll have to pay your own tuition. I chose the Catholic option and paid my own way through high school.

So being able to work hard and maybe even suffer through some of the things I went through came fairly easily to me, having watched how much my parents suffered through each day to ensure their children had the best educations they could get. How much less stress would my parents have felt if they had been less passionate about us getting an education? Tons! But they had their convictions, and man, did they rub off.

Having started working at an early age and learning its value was something I was able to carry forward throughout my adult life. So what did working hard each day teach me about finding my passion? That if I wanted something bad enough, I was going to have to pay a price to get it, and that might mean suffering to some degree.

Work & Vocation

Are you passionate about your work? Most people work a nine-to-five job to earn their money and pay their bills. They may save a little and use some for entertainment. They get up in the morning, put in their eight hours, clock out, and then head home for dinner and family time. There is nothing wrong with that. Maybe that person puts in his time and has a hobby he comes home to that he is passionate about. There are entrepreneurs or business owners out there who do their work, put in their time, maybe even fifty to seventy hours a week, make their money, and still go home unfulfilled. When people tell me they are passionate about their work, I always ask this question: If you were not getting paid to do this work, would you still do it? If their answer is yes, then I would say they are passionate about what they do.

I love my work, but I am not passionate about real estate. I am passionate about what real estate can do for me and others. I am passionate about helping others, and real estate is a means by which I can help others all day every day. I help people buy and sell homes. During that process, there are challenges that usually show up along the way. I love trying to solve those problems to assist people in getting to the closing. But if you were to ask me, "Rob, if you were not getting paid to sell real estate, would you still do it?" my answer may come as a surprise. It is an emphatic "no." Real estate is not my passion.

So why do I bother?

If I told you the answer was "for the money," would you be disappointed? Okay, maybe it's not for the money exactly, but for the things money can buy. Sounds materialistic, huh, kind of heartless even? But hear me out.

The money my real estate agency generates allows me to do something else I love: provide for others, and I provide for them in ways that have nothing to do with the business of real estate. Whether it's hosting a client appreciation party or sponsoring a school team's sports uniforms or giving my son the funds to pay his rent at college so he can pursue his dream of becoming a meteorologist, money allows me to help others achieve their goals, or at the very least, pay for things that provide an enjoyable experience or fulfill material needs and wants.

So, it makes sense then that since I love providing for others—kind of like a dad does—I picked a profession that would put me in a stable enough position to help others. But even providing for the needs of others isn't my true passion. That's just a perk of having a decent job.

For me, it's less about helping others succeed financially and more about inspiring people to become the best versions of themselves.

A Passionate Marriage

The numbers from the American Psychological Association suggest that 40 to 50 percent of marriages end in divorce. Why is that? There are a number of reasons, and I would guess one of the most common reasons marriages end in divorce is a lack of communication. There are many others, of course, but the question I have is this: Are you willing to suffer for the success of your marriage?

Where am I going with this? Young adults tend to think once you get married, it's all glory and bliss. Sure, there is the honeymoon, the intimacy, and the excitement of being newlyweds, but to keep a marriage going, a couple has to work. And for a marriage to last, couples have to work hard. There will be struggles along the way, but marriage is a journey.

One time my wife and I were struggling with something. We hadn't been communicating well. I went to church one morning and I was thinking about the Passion of Christ. A light bulb went off! I thought, *Well, what about the passion of my marriage?* That evening as my wife and I were having a conversation, I brought up this topic. I talked to her about this epiphany I'd had with regard to the Passion of Christ and how it can relate to a marriage. Marriage isn't just a one-way ride of good feelings, love, sex, and whatever else comes to mind. Some of the struggles you encounter along the way are greater than others. Some are minor, and some are intense.

Those struggles can consist of communication, finances, career, and so forth. You get the idea. When going through those struggles, if you think about how much you want the marriage to succeed and are willing to work through and embrace those struggles, they won't seem so bad.

Passionate for the Sport and the Win

When I was a child, I was passionate about sports, particularly baseball. At five years old I wanted to be a baseball player and I would sacrifice anything to be out on the field. I would tell my friends to go ahead without me when they were on their way somewhere else. Later, in high school, on several occasions I did not join friends when they would go on a ski trip or another adventure. All I wanted to do was play baseball.

I had to work extremely hard at baseball because I wasn't a big kid and I didn't have much of an arm. But I was determined and tenacious. I would walk across the street every other day to the school grounds. At the far end of the yard stood the gymnasium with a large brick wall, no windows, and a steel door. I would stand fifteen or twenty feet from the wall and toss the ball against it for a few minutes to loosen up; then I would gradually move farther and farther away from the wall so that I would have to throw the ball longer distances. The idea was that the long toss would strengthen my arm over time. Eventually, I could stand about two hundred feet from the wall and hit it at a low angle. After that, I focused on the steel door as a target to improve my accuracy. I put a lot of dents in that door. I did this for months and months. My passion bordered on the obsessive.

I went on to play baseball in college, and there was a point in time when I thought I would go pro, but it never happened. I was injured and my dreams were dashed. Still, I look back at that time as me exhibiting my best youthful self. I would do whatever was necessary to get better because by doing all the work, I was becoming not only a better athlete, but also a more disciplined and focused individual. I had the tools to solve problems that would come along. I could look at a new challenge and trust myself to tackle it. The physical discipline made me a more strategic and balanced thinker.

I also played basketball as a kid. I played on a school team up until the ninth grade. I never thought about coaching the sport until my younger daughter, Amanda, began playing in the fourth grade. Originally, all I wanted to do was to help out her team as an assistant to the coach, but two years after she started playing, I found myself the head coach for her team.

I didn't know what I was doing initially, but I fell in love with it. No surprise, I read a book about coaching girls' basketball, followed the suggestions, and soon enough I was jumping up and down on the sidelines like a madman. I became passionate about the girls playing well, and I loved seeing them improve game after game. I admit that because I was always so darn competitive, I was passionate about them winning too.

I used to think coaches were a little overboard when they got excited on the sidelines during a game. I remember watching the Maryland Terrapins play when Gary Williams was coach. By half-time each game, his coat was off and he was sweating profusely. I thought, *This is ridiculous*—until I experienced it myself.

The game moves fast. There is an intensity that's hard to describe except to say that you just get caught up in the moment. I would find myself in my own little bubble, not worrying about what others thought of me or what I looked like. I didn't have any other care in the world except for what was happening in front of me. The immediacy was primal.

I remember one night my wife, my son, and I were sitting in the first row at midcourt. Amanda's team was losing by twelve points in the fourth quarter. Then, they mounted this crazy comeback and were down by only two points with under a minute to play. My daughter stole the ball and started her breakaway up court, only to hear the shot clock buzzer sound. I think every girl on the court stopped what they were doing, including my daughter. I saw the screeching halt happening right in front of me. As I watched Amanda pull up to stop her dribble because of the buzzer, I jumped out of my seat, almost onto the court, and yelled to her, "Go! Go! Go!" My cell phone went flying onto the court and tore apart into three pieces. Amanda registered me yelling at her, kicked it back into gear, and drove down the court. Unfortunately, we didn't convert the breakaway into a basket. We lost the game. But hell if that wasn't one of the most invigorating moments I was able to experience with my daughter and her teammates.

Afterward, my wife and some of the nearby fans were laughing at me and commenting about how crazy I looked while I was yelling at Amanda. I shrugged and replied, "That's what happens when you are in the moment." On the way home, even I was laughing at myself at the thought of what I must have looked like to everyone as I jumped out of my seat.

Passion brings intensity. When people are passionate, they become hyper-focused to get a job done and to get it done with excellence. When people are truly passionate, they are intentional about what they're doing, even if they occasionally look like they've lost all sense of themselves.

But there's a fine line here. Being passionate doesn't mean you have to act like a madman or break your stuff purely for some pleasure-seeking satisfaction. Plenty of "passionate" people go off the rails because they are consumed by a goal but lack a foundation. They haven't put down their roots.

Conversely, there are also many dispassionate people who never get excited about anything. They may be grounded, but I will bet with confidence that they are rarely inspired. They haven't found their calling, and they aren't living their purpose.

We sometimes wonder why we treat athletes as heroes. We question why they get paid so much just to play sports. But the truth is sports are among the best demonstrations of a committed passion. Rarely does someone who doesn't absolutely love what he or she does excel at sports. That's because in order to be good at sports, you have to commit to yourself and set that foundation. You have to manage the mundane—developing skills and building routines and repeating behaviors over and over again. But in the process, you become attuned to your physical place in space. You become aware of how small changes cause major rippling impacts; you are secure about decisions you make, and you know with clarity and consideration whether you feel fulfilled. And hopefully, with all that work behind you, during that game, you feel an extraordinary sense of accomplishment. And the fans appreciate the effort.

It's funny. I used to tell my kids to be more aggressive in sports, to not shy away from trusting their skills and abilities. They wouldn't, though—become more aggressive, that is. I suspect it was a question of passion. With confidence comes a more assertive attitude, and in sports in particular that attitude translates into actions.

Conversely, we hesitate when we are unsure about our potential for success or our commitment to following a path that we're treading. And if we're not sure, it's important that we check for our passion and decide whether we want to keep going down the path we're on, or we want to seek out something extraordinary to us.

How to Discover Your Passion

As I mentioned earlier, when I began reading and having those conversations that elevated my energy to another level, that's when I knew I was on to something. What are you doing in your life that causes you to feel that energy rise to a different level? Is it something in your work? Perhaps it's in your marriage or raising your family? Maybe it's in a hobby that you have? Pay close attention to the ideas that come to mind and make your heart beat faster. Spend some quiet time consistently and listen to that voice that's guiding you along the way. Pray for discernment to know when that moment arrives. The voice is talking to you, and it's there all the time. Listen to it, feel it in your heart, and trust it's taking you where you need to go.

So ask yourself: Do you desire to live a fulfilling life? Are you willing to live with passion? I often use the example of Sir William Wallace in the movie *Braveheart*. He was willing to die for his men, for his country, and for his land. He was passionate about leading his people to *freedom!* Are you willing to do the same? I'm not speaking literally, but figuratively. Are you willing to let your false-self die to live the life you're truly supposed to live? Are you passionate about being the best version of yourself? Live with passion and no matter what happens in life, you will live a life fulfilled.

So many people live their lives desiring to be someone else. They want to be like Mike (Michael Jordan) as the saying goes. Why would you want to be anyone else besides yourself? Be aware of that humming in your heart when you're experiencing or reading something. It's a clue to what your calling or purpose in life may be. You must learn to follow your heart, find your purpose, and follow your passion!

SECTION III

UNDERSTANDING WHAT YOU ALREADY HAVE

CHAPTER 10

SEASONS OF LIFE:
KNOWING WHAT SEASON YOU'RE IN

EVERYONE GOES THROUGH their own seasons
of life. We can easily look back in hindsight and see when we went
through a season. How meaningful would it be to become aware
of a season you're in when you're actually going through it or
when you know you're about to go through it?

There are many seasons in our lives. We can experience seasons in our friendships, family relationships, businesses, parenting, and even in our own ways of thinking and our belief systems.
When we can acknowledge these seasons or become aware of
them, it makes us appreciate the season we're in at any given time
and find more joy in those times.

Relationships Have Seasons

In 2002 I joined Toastmasters. Toastmasters is an international organization for those who want to polish their public speaking skills.
A Toastmasters event consists of several segments in which one can

participate to practice the art of speaking. More importantly, you can attend a Toastmasters event to learn how to become a better listener. God gave us two ears and one mouth for a reason.

One night at a Toastmasters meeting, a fellow speaker named Karen talked about the seasons of friendships. What she said that night really stuck with me, and I want to share it with you.

To summarize, she said that over the course of your lifetime, you will make hundreds of acquaintances. When you're young, everyone is your friend. You have friends as a child, as a teenager, as a young adult. Later, you build more mature friendships as an elderly person. Life is about relationships, and in every part of our lives we have the opportunity to establish them, and in some instances, turn those associations into friendships. But friendships have their seasons, like the seasons themselves. They come and they go. Sometimes they last for years, yet other times they are brief. All relationships end at some point simply because they run their course.

I related her speech to the friendships you build as a parent while your children are going through school. Most of these acquaintances last as long as your child attends that school. When your child moves from one school to another, some relationships end and new ones begin. Parents associate with the parents of the kids their children are associating with, especially if they are involved in sports or other activities. Parents have a natural opportunity to connect with each other in this environment.

Debbie and I had been associated with the elementary school my children attended for ten years or so. My wife and I had developed some really close friends throughout our time there, and for that, we were extremely grateful. When my son graduated from elementary school to move on to high school, we knew we were not going to see some of the parents we had been associating with for so long.

When a season like this comes to end, it brings a sense of sadness. It's okay to be sad, but life goes on. There are new people to meet and new experiences to be had. Sometimes when seasons end or change, people don't handle the change well. When relationships run their course and come to an end, we can feel hurt, emotional, or even resentful. We spend entirely too much time and energy feeling sorry for ourselves because a friendship has come to an end.

The importance of Karen's speech that night was to describe what we should do instead of being sad, or hurt, or even resentful. Instead, we should be thankful for the time that person was in our lives. We should be thankful for what we learned, what we shared, and all the experiences we had with that person. When we are grateful, good things happen. When we are resentful or hurting, we attract negative emotions.

I completely agree with this powerful message. But I didn't always understand it so well.

Letting Go of a Relationship

Growing up, I had a lot of friends. From the time I was thirteen until the time I was in my thirties, I had a core group of friends who stuck together through everything. We were a tight-knit group for at least twenty years. One of my closest friends in that group, Jimmy, was the best man in my wedding. A few years after getting married, Jimmy and I took on a real estate project. We bought a foreclosed property in South Baltimore with the idea of renovating it and reselling it.

We bought the property in my name, and the goal was for him to invest his money in renovations up to the point of what I spent to purchase the property. From that point on, all monies would come out of each of our pockets at a 50/50 rate. We were both excited about this venture. Best friends, living the American dream of investing money, working hard, and building wealth. Things started out great, but as time wore on, things began going sideways. We weren't on the same page as to how much time each of us should be spending at the property during the renovations. The biggest mistake we made from the beginning was not defining in writing both of our roles in the venture. You would think there is nothing that could ever come between you and your best friend, but there is. Money!

We finished the project, marketed the house, and eventually sold it. But there was tension between us as things came to a close. Months went by before we spoke again. It was painful for me and I assume for him as well. It was uncomfortable for our wives, too. One day my wife suggested I reach out to Jimmy to clear the air. As painful as it was to lose my best friend over a business transaction, which netted each of us about ten thousand dollars, I realized I was beginning to resent him too. I wanted to get together to apologize for my part in this deal not going well (when things don't go well in any type of relationship, all parties involved play a part in it), and I also wanted to apologize for starting to resent my best friend.

We got together for lunch a few weeks later. My expectation was that we were going to get together, clear the air, say our apologies, and then end it with a big buddy hug and everything would go back to normal, just like old times. Wrong! We ate lunch, chatted a bit, and then got down to the point of why we were there. It turns out he blamed me for all that had happened. I was in shock! I still moved forward with my apologies, hoping things were going to get better, but they didn't. We were not going to get through this as I had hoped.

We didn't speak for almost six years. Of course, we would see each other in passing because we had so many friends in common, but we did our best to ignore each other. I can only speak for myself, but the pain of losing my best friend and not even talking to each other for all that time was immense. I would wake up day after day hurting over the loss. I was almost depressed over it. Some mornings I would shake my head, wondering where it all went wrong. Other mornings I would wake up with resentment and anger, not caring if I ever spoke to him again.

Then one fateful day, I heard my friend Karen give her speech at that Toastmasters meeting. I had never taken the time to be grateful for all the great years Jimmy and I had spent together as friends because I was too busy feeling sorry for myself and being resentful of him. Our friendship had enjoyed its season. Now it was time for each of our seasons of life to change. We had a great run as really good friends, and for that, I was thankful. What I did next was life-changing for me then, and something I still do up until this day.

I had learned the skill of journaling years earlier and knew how therapeutic it was for me. So I pulled out my journal and wrote my old friend a letter. I wrote the letter asking forgiveness for my role in the situation, thanking him for all the great years we had together, and finally, wishing him and his family all the best. There was so much emotion in that letter! I never sent it because that was never my plan. The idea of writing the letter was to get all the hurt and thoughts about what had happened out of my head and to let them go. I had been holding on to the hurt way too long, and I needed to release it. I can't begin to tell you how relieved I was when I was finished. I was going to miss all those good times we shared, and I knew things were never going to be the same. But I wasn't going to let myself hurt anymore. I was able to let that season pass, grateful for the friendship while it lasted, and not resentful that it was now lost.

If I hadn't gone to Toastmasters that evening and heard Karen give her speech, I don't know if I would have ever learned the skill or the art of appreciating a friendship for its season. I am now able to go into all my friendships knowing they have a season. I'm not thinking about when the relationship will end, but I am able to appreciate it as it evolves.

Reflect on your life and think about any friendships that have fallen by the wayside. As painful as it may have been, can you now see the good in those relationships? Take a moment to journal those experiences and then feel the appreciation for the season you had with that person. Be grateful for the good memories and let go of any bitterness you have. This frees you from any inner turmoil you may be going through, and it allows you to be more present in the current season you're in.

Rites of Passage

Think of the season of parenting. You get married and have children. You raise your children in your household for eighteen, twenty, twenty-five (and hopefully not thirty) years. One day, they realize it's time for them to leave, or you wake up and realize it's time to send them on their way. If you have left home, or have had children who have left home, particularly to go out of state, saying goodbye can be an extremely painful experience. We need to be thankful for all those years of rewards and challenges spent together, and then let go. I know it's not easy, but when we come from a place of gratitude, life can be so much better.

Some call it a rite of passage. I call it a blessing or simply a great experience. You bring your child up in a world of unknowns and do the best you can. From their birth to watching them walk for the first time, to riding a bike, to getting their driver's license, to going off to school, and to getting married, we are fortunate to be able to experience all these events in our lifetime as a parent. I don't think you ever know how you are going to respond to one of these rites of passage until it happens. When it does, it's a special kind of feeling and a great memory.

I think about when my children got their driver's licenses. It felt like they went from young children to having to take on the huge responsibility of driving overnight. I think about when they purchased their first car. They went from the season of depending on us for rides all the time to experiencing independence. They experienced their rite of passage going from young children to responsible teenagers. Standing by as a parent and being aware of this happening brought so much joy and fulfillment in my life.

When my wife I were first married we didn't have the responsibility of having children yet, so we lived a different lifestyle. Once we decided to have children, our season changed. We experienced our own rite of passage to becoming parents. Rites of passage are like going through a door of the known to the unknown.

The Doors of Life

We see them every day. We walk through them every day. We open them. We close them. Sometimes we knock on them. Sometimes others knock on ours. What is it about doors that strike a chord with me?

Several years back, my son attended a leadership camp in Boston. It was the first time a child in our family had gone away to a camp, getting on a plane and not knowing one person at his destination. A daunting experience, yes!

My son was an anxious kid—like so many. The idea of doing something new or competing in a sports event unnerved him to the point where he would always hesitate. It's almost like he couldn't take action. Yet, he had made the decision to attend the camp. For two months approaching the day of departure, we saw no signs of anxiety, which quite frankly, surprised me. This wasn't like Robbie. *Maybe we are past this anxiety thing*, I thought. Finally, the day arrived, and our son was leaving for Boston. It was early in the morning that summer day, and we had to hurry to make the flight. Just before leaving, I wanted to say a prayer together as a family. We stood around the kitchen island and said our prayer. I looked up, and suddenly I could see the stress on Robbie's face. He literally released his emotions in that moment. Soon enough, all of us broke out in tears.

When Robbie made the decision to go, I had decided to accompany him. I planned to leave him with his group and then spend the day with a good friend of mine. We flew to Boston, arrived at the baggage claim area, where we met a representative of the organization who would be leading us to a designated place where a bus would be picking up my son to take him to his home for the next six days. As we stood waiting for our luggage, my wife called me: "How is he doing?"

I responded, "He's doing fine, but I'm not." I suddenly broke down in tears as I let my emotions get the best of me. I was letting my thirteen-year-old son go on his own with people we didn't know for the next week—a rite of passage for us both.

We grabbed our luggage and headed out to the area where we were to meet the bus to pick up my son. After an hour of waiting and a huge build-up of anxiety for both of us, the bus arrived. It parked, and a woman stepped out.

"You must be Dad?" she said.

"I certainly am," I responded. After some small talk, she looked at me and while pointing her finger at me, said, "Get a good look at his face now, because after a week, it's going to change!"

Hearing that, I lost it. I grabbed my son and gave him a huge hug. We hugged about as hard as we ever had and cried together like we had never done before.

But it was time to say goodbye. He turned toward the bus, walking away from me, and took what I assume were two very scary and intimidating steps onto the bus. He was out of my sight and would be on his own for a week. I instantly captured that picture in my mind and will forever remember that moment. It reminded me of the movie *Field of Dreams* when the players left the field at the end of the day, walked into the cornfields, and disappeared.

How many times a day do we walk through doors, literally? To leave our house, to go from one room to the next, to walk into our place of business, to go into stores, restaurants, and so on. The moment my son stepped through the door of that bus, his life changed, as did mine. I'm sure he was scared to death, but it took courage to keep moving forward despite his fear. Whenever we approach a door in our lives, we can't be 100 percent sure what lays on the other side. We have to approach those doors regardless of our fear and enter with courage. Every decision we make in life is like approaching a doorway. We have a choice to make, and each choice represents a passage. We're not absolutely sure what consequences our choices will have, but we still have to keep moving forward, despite that fear of the unknown. Our lives move in different directions all the time dictated by the choices we make, the doors we decide to open, and the doors we decide to close.

Six days later, we picked my son up at the airport. As he walked off that plane, all I wanted to do was see his face and the change that had occurred in those last six days. And change I saw! I saw confidence! I saw happiness! I saw a changed little boy, my son!

Whenever we make pivotal decisions in life, we become that changed little boy. We walk away with confidence from those decisions. We walk away happier we have made a choice! We walk away changed! I was inspired by that moment, and every time I have to make a decision in life, I think of that day and the courage my son had to have to take those two steps into the unknown. He inspired me that day and for the rest of my days!

We experience multiple types of seasons in our lives. The gift is to recognize them and appreciate them in the moment, and to walk through the door from one season to the next.

REFLECTION QUESTIONS

- **What seasons of life have you experienced?**
- **What fulfillment have you enjoyed by experiencing your rites of passage or watching those close to you experience theirs?**
- **Were you bitter when the season ended, or were you grateful for the season itself?**

CHAPTER 11

BE AWARE
OF THE BLESSINGS IN YOUR LIFE

WHAT'S THE FIRST QUESTION people ask when they run into or call one another? The majority of the time I would bet it's "How are you?" Typical answers are "I'm doing great," "Couldn't be better," or "No use in complaining." My favorite answer, which I'm hearing more and more, is "I'm blessed" or "I'm so blessed." I love this answer for the simple reason that we *are* all blessed in so many ways. Most of the time our blessings are directly in front of us, but we don't recognize them for what they are. However, when we practice awareness, we are better able to recognize them, and then we get to experience that sense of joy and fulfillment that we all long for.

My Wife

Back when I was in grade school, there was a family whose children, two girls, had recently started attending our school. They were not only the new kids on the block; they were from England.

How did a family from England end up in Northeast Baltimore at our school? we all wondered.

At one point, my younger brother dated the younger sister for a short period of time. We were in grade school together, so I knew of the older sister, Debbie, but never developed any kind of relationship with her. We graduated from grade school, and Debbie went to the Catholic all-girls high school, about a half mile from the Catholic boys' school I attended. We graduated from our respective high schools, and I went on to college in Florida while she began her career in Baltimore.

A year after I graduated from college, I left Florida to return home. I took a job at a local investment company, T. Rowe Price, in downtown Baltimore. Each morning, I drove from my house to park on the street across from the grade school I had attended years earlier and then walk down to a bus stop to catch the bus to go to work. After work, I walked several blocks to catch the bus for my ride home.

The first day I got on the bus to come home from work, I recognized an attractive girl sitting near the front. It was Debbie, the older sister who had come to Baltimore from England. I knew who she was but didn't think for a second she would recognize me. As fate would have it, we both left the bus at the same stop, just a few blocks from where I was parked and another two blocks from where she lived. We got off the bus and walked five blocks next to each other without saying a word. This went on for weeks.

It was a snowy, frigid Saturday night in January. I was celebrating a good friend of mine's twenty-fifth birthday at a gathering in a local bar. No sooner had I walked in than I noticed Debbie sitting at a table with some of her friends. Soon enough, we crossed paths and engaged in a conversation of almost two hours. I wasn't worried so much about hanging around my buddies as I was interested in this beautiful woman. After two hours of great conversation, I decided I would ask her out. Thinking it was a slam dunk, I was shocked when she initially said no. She told me I wouldn't remember any of the conversation the next day because we were drinking. I saw this as an opportunity to prove her wrong.

Two nights later, on my way out with my friend Ken, I asked him if we could swing by Debbie's house so I could drop something off on her porch. She was working that night so I knew she wouldn't be home. Earlier in the day, I had purchased a single rose in a box, and I put the rose on the porch with a note that read, "Here's my number. Call me and give me your phone number so I can call you back and ask you out." Two hours later, I received a phone call from her and her first words were, "Will you marry me?" Four and a half years later, we were married and now have been married for over twenty years.

Debbie has been a huge blessing in my life and is the rock of our family. She allows me to work hard to provide for our family while she manages the household. She has raised our children and makes sure they are prepared for school. She has always made sure they were where they needed to be on time, whether it was school or a doctor's appointment. Debbie is the person I come home to every night and allows me to talk to her. I'm able to lean into her, love her, and spend time with her. We are not only husband and wife; we are best friends!

My Children and the Unexpected Blessings They Bring

As a father, I always dream of my children understanding the things I do. Often as parents, we advise our kids on how to be successful when they grow up. We try to guide them the best way we know how. We repeat ourselves often and wonder, *Why don't they listen to me?*

The answer is this: Our children are so busy watching what we do that they can't hear what we are saying. They do what we do and not what we advise. We set examples for our children all the time, and we get frustrated when we tell our kids the same thing several times and they don't listen.

Our children are mirrors of who we are. As a dad, I always looked forward to my son doing the things I had done. I tried to encourage my son to play baseball as a child and teenager because that was my favorite sport. In fact, I was always encouraging him to play all sports because I was a sports enthusiast. Sports were my life, and I wanted them to be his life. I believed sons grew up to do what their dads did and daughters grew up doing what their moms did. Boy, was I wrong!

Not only would I encourage him to play sports all the time, I would try to get him to read. I love to read, so it only made sense that my son would have the same desire to read. Wrong again.

As Robbie and Amanda have grown up, I've discovered Robbie likes sports and plays them well, but he doesn't *love* sports like I do. He's a brilliant student. He likes the weather and has been interested in meteorology since he was five years old. Knowing all this, I still continued to force sports on him. One day, we got into a heated discussion, and he totally caught me off guard and blessed me with a huge gift. After I had pushed baseball once more, he interrupted me and said, "Dad, I don't love sports like you. I love the weather!"

My jaw dropped. He was 100 percent correct, and I knew it. He humbled me and blessed me at the same time. I should have been able to see he just didn't have a passion for sports as I did. And that's okay. I had loved baseball since I was five. I should have seen his love for the weather since he was five. In fact, I *did* see it, but I ignored it for my own selfish reasons. Robbie helped me see it wasn't about what I wanted for him; it was more about what he wanted for himself. Going forward, I realized I had to do things for him and coach him in what he was passionate about.

Then there is Amanda, my youngest daughter who, at an early age, told my wife and me how much she loved soccer. She did not display much skill as a young player, but she continued to play and to get better. Eventually, Amanda became a leader on the team. She played defense in soccer, and her ability to defend was second to none. In addition, she played basketball at a high level, recreational lacrosse, and was on the local swimming team. Amanda always wanted to be outside playing sports.

I never pushed Amanda, and she continued to do what she loved to do. I continued to push Robbie, and it was almost as if it backfired on me. I love both Robbie and Amanda equally, and I have learned to let them follow their hearts and their dreams.

Almost the same situation occurred with the reading. One evening I came home to find Amanda and Debbie engaged in what seemed to be an exciting conversation. Amanda included me as she shared her plan regarding her future. I was impressed by her thinking at thirteen years old. She was talking about things like helping the poor and the homeless, feeding the hungry, and traveling the world to accomplish these things. I was touched and excited for her. Later that evening, as I sat in my home office doing some work, Amanda walked in with a little bounce in her step and, gesturing at all my bookshelves, asked me, "Is this where you get all your inspiration and motivation?"

"You could say that," I said. "In fact, as long as you live in this house, you will never have to go to a Barnes and Nobles to purchase a book." She laughed, looked around, and asked me to pick a book for her to read. As you can imagine, my heart was melting.

I picked a book, *The Seed* by Jon Gordon, and gave it to her. She then asked me if I could get her a journal as well. Now my heart was really melting! "What are you going to do with a journal?" I asked.

"I'm going to write about all the people I'm going to help in my life and all the things I'm going to do and places I plan to go."

Wow! She continued to tug at my heart. I had two brand-new journals sitting on my desk, and I asked her if she wanted one. She said no, because she would rather have one with a string that you can tie around the journal just like the very first one I'd had. She knew specifically what she wanted.

She said she was going to start reading *The Seed* that night. It was already 10:30, and it was a school night. I told her she had to get to bed. Her response was this: "Dad, when I go to bed at night, I never fall right to sleep. I'm too busy thinking. Reading helps me go to sleep." I was speechless. I looked at her and smiled.

When Amanda awoke the next morning, I asked her if she had read any of the book, and if so, what she had learned from it. She had read seven chapters, and she told me three things she learned that night. *Follow your heart. Find your purpose. Follow your passion.* That's a powerful response to get from a thirteen-year-old who read her first seven chapters of a personal growth book the night before. I couldn't have been more proud of her. On her own, she had decided to ask me to pick a book for her to read and she decided to begin journaling. This was a blessing indeed.

A few months went by, and Amanda had read seven books by then. We were off to a soccer tournament that upcoming weekend. We were in the second of two games, and to reach the championship game, we would have to win this game. Regulation time ended in a tie, but no ties were allowed at this point, so the game would go into penalty kicks. Amanda would be the fourth shooter for her team. When it came time for her to take her penalty kick, we were leading 2-1. Amanda set the ball, backed up, and then approached the ball to shoot. In a calm and cool manner, she struck the ball and scored. Of course, we were ecstatic Amanda scored the game-winning goal, but this moment wasn't about her scoring the winning goal. I put my arm around her shoulders and asked if she had been nervous. Without hesitation she replied, "No!"

Then I asked her, "What was going through your mind as you approached the ball to shoot?"

"I was thinking about all those books I have been reading the last few months." Tears of joy filled my eyes as I thought about how powerful that statement was. My daughter was catching more from me than she was hearing. It was a blessing and a gift!

As parents, we work on raising our children as best we can, and we may repeat ourselves over and over, sometimes thinking our children will never understand the things we try to teach them. And then one day, out of nowhere, it clicks for them. For years I had been suggesting to my children the importance of reading and I would continually try to encourage them to read. The night Amanda came into my room asking me to pick a book for her to read, and then months later telling me why she had felt confidence in the moment she had, filled my heart with joy. It made me realize the fulfillment and joy we seek from the lessons we try to teach our children don't always come when we would like them to, but they will come if we persevere as parents.

Crystal

I was sixteen when I first learned I was going to be a father. My girlfriend at the time was fifteen. I was raised by a devout Catholic mother and grew up with the Catholic teaching not to have premarital sex, so perhaps more than usual I was riddled with guilt at the thought of letting my parents down. But I knew one thing for sure: I was going to take responsibility for my actions.

My girlfriend and I had broken up before my daughter Crystal was born, but as I said, I was not going to hide from my responsibilities. About a week into my senior year of high school, on September 12, 1984, I officially became a dad. I was a scared seventeen-year-old, as I am sure Crystal's mom, Regina, was a frightened sixteen-year-old. I planned to finish high school, go to the local community college, and then get a job to support my daughter.

The day after Crystal was born, I thought it would be best for me to talk to a priest at school to let him know what was going on in my life. I went to my English teacher, Fr. Jude Michael, and explained the situation. He listened to my every word with compassion. When we were finished, he told me, "Since you came to me in confidence, I will not say anything to anyone. If the principal finds out, you could get kicked out of school." Great information to hear your first week of school your senior year!

That certainly added another layer of stress to my life! As I went through my senior year of high school full of anxiety, I did the best I could to keep it quiet. My closest friends knew of my becoming a father, but if someone ever mentioned it, I had to deny it as a rumor. I feared being expelled from school. I am a devout Catholic and I always will be, but life does happen and God does have mercy. I could not understand kicking a seventeen-year-old out of school when what he needed most was compassion, not punishment. But the Catholic Church forbids premarital sex, and since I attended a Catholic school, and it was obvious I had sex before marriage, they would have expelled me for that.

It was a tough senior year, and there were challenges along the way. I was getting up at 4:00 a.m. to earn money so I could pay my tuition and help raise my daughter, who lived a few miles away. In addition, I had to work hard to keep my grades up. But I prayed hard every night and every morning for everyone involved and for me to be the best father I could be.

For two and a half years after my daughter's birth, I went to her house to visit a couple times a week. I would take diapers, baby food, clothes, and whatever I could afford to give her in addition to a small money order to help with the finances. I hoped to obtain at least an A.A. degree to enhance my résumé when applying for a future job.

As I've mentioned, as my sophomore year of college came to an end, I was offered an opportunity to play baseball at FAU in Boca Raton, Florida. But I had a responsibility at home. I was nineteen at the time and was presented this great opportunity. Yes, it could be viewed as selfish for me to go, but there was also the opportunity to get my four-year college degree and better myself for everyone involved. It would require two years away from home and Crystal. It was a tough decision for any kid that age, but because of my responsibility, there was added pressure.

After much thought and conversation, I decided to accept the offer. I would have a four-year degree, and potentially better employment and income. Admittedly, I would also get to play baseball, my dream. I could do more for my daughter by completing my education away from home. I wrote a letter to Crystal's mom explaining the entire situation.

It was August 24, 1987, when I drove away from the only place I had ever called home. Within a couple weeks of my arrival, I received a letter from Crystal's mom that wasn't very pleasant. She basically told me to stay out of their life and never come back. On my first visit home from school, I spoke to a lawyer, who told me it was better to stay away. I didn't have the money to pursue any type of custody, and if I attempted to see Crystal, her mother could call the police and have me arrested. It was a tough situation to be in, but it was something I had to face.

I had to put the situation in the back of my mind. In my heart, I knew I would see my daughter again. I just didn't know when. I stayed in Florida for four years: three to finish school, and one to explore it as a possible permanent location if things were not going to work out back home. In October 1991, I decided it was time to come home. I had graduated with a B.S. degree in finance and the hope of landing a nice job in Baltimore. I also hoped for an opportunity to see my daughter, but I still couldn't force the issue.

Not long after arriving home, I met my future wife. I told Debbie about Crystal as soon as we began dating, so there would be no surprises. We had been together for about three years when I received a call from my mom one evening. She called to tell me that Crystal had found out about me and wanted to meet me. Her mom had been dating another guy and had three other children. I assumed Crystal grew up believing that guy was her dad. At ten years old she discovered that not to be true and asked her mom if she could meet me.

There was no question in my mind it was time to take responsibility and be the dad I was supposed to be ten years earlier. As scary as it was for me, I'm sure it was ten times scarier for Crystal. We agreed on a date to meet, and I saw my daughter for the first time since she was two and a half years old. After I knocked on the door of her mother's home, Regina answered, and then Crystal came to the door. I can't really put into words what that moment was like except to say it was special.

I experienced excitement seeing my daughter for the first time in seven-plus years, but I also experienced guilt for not being there in all that time. In that moment, however, it didn't matter. I was her father, she was my daughter, and we were reunited.

For the next few years, we would talk from week to week, and then go several weeks without contact. I had to keep in mind that I was a twenty-seven-year-old stranger who walked into her life when she was only ten years old. I totally understood any discomfort she felt and the gaps in our contact.

Finally, when Crystal was thirteen, things suddenly clicked. Despite being thirteen, she looked like she was sixteen or seventeen. It was a Sunday afternoon, and I had planned to take Crystal to an Orioles game. Earlier that morning I had a conversation with Debbie in which I said that I thought I was going to be humbled at the game. I didn't know how, but I just had a feeling. We arrived at the game to find out it was "Poster Day" and any child thirteen years or younger would get a Cal Ripken poster. Of course, we were both excited. I was taking my daughter to her first Orioles game and she was getting a Cal Ripken poster. We approached the man to get our poster, and I asked him for one for my daughter. He looked at me, glanced at her, then back at me and said, "C'mon dude, that's jailbait!"

I was stunned! I thought about the conversation I'd had with Debbie earlier. I took one step past the gentleman and thought about how this moment came to be. *Should I respond at all? Or accept it for what it was and move on?* I decided to address the situation. I took one step back, and I literally put my finger up to the gentleman's chin. I said, "She's my daughter, she is thirteen years old, and don't you *ever* talk to anyone like that again! Now give her a poster." The guy looked at me with fear in his eyes and asked me to relax. He gave Crystal a poster. We looked at each other, smiled, and then I asked her why she had to look so much older. We both laughed and then enjoyed the game. That was the day things came together for us.

A couple of years after our bonding moment, Crystal started helping me with my newspaper business, from an administrative side. She had gotten her driver's license and came over to my house after school to log the billing for my newspaper customers into the system. She ran reports and printed lists for me. I was fortunate to see her more often because of my business. The time we spent together strengthened our relationship.

Crystal graduated high school and then attended college. I explained to her how important I thought it was to live on campus or at the dorms to really experience the college life. I had been eleven hundred miles from home during college, and she was going to be about ten miles from home. But the miles were not as important as simply being out on her own. Just before her freshman year, we moved her into an apartment near where the students stayed. I told her how excited I was for her, and I couldn't wait for her to tell me all her college stories.

Well, that wasn't going to be.

One evening while she was at my home working, Crystal told me she had something to discuss. She had been dating a neighborhood guy for a while prior to going to college, and while really not feeling the college life, she decided to move in with her boyfriend's family. Of course, this was something I didn't approve of, but I looked at her admission as another opportunity to bond with my daughter.

Crystal had her own car, but it was registered in my name, and I paid the auto insurance. I told her that although I wasn't going to agree with her moving in with her boyfriend's family, I would be willing to make a compromise. The deal would be that if something were to happen to the car because it was in a place I thought it shouldn't be (her boyfriend's house), we were going to register the car in her name and she was going to pay the car insurance. If she was willing to agree to these terms, then I would not say any more about it. She agreed. Giving her the opportunity to make her own decision and not coming off like a dictator dad allowed Crystal and I to respect each other's feelings.

Four years later, I was able to watch my daughter walk

across the stage to receive her diploma from Villa Julie College in Baltimore County, Maryland. I must have been the youngest dad there—or at least the dad with the darkest hair (most dads had either lost their hair by then or it had turned gray). Crystal graduated and started her working career at Toyota Credit Corp. Then the next big event came to pass. Crystal planned to get married, and I would be walking my daughter down the aisle to hand her off to her new husband.

Ten years earlier, I would have never imagined being so blessed. Wow! It was a special day for me and for Crystal as well, and a moment of awe. My reunion with my older daughter showed me that God works in ways that we sometimes cannot comprehend, but we have to trust in His plan for us.

Although becoming a father at age seventeen may sound like a negative, I now believe I was truly blessed. I was blessed with a beautiful daughter. I was blessed with faith. Not being able to see her for all those years was tough, and thinking there was a possibility I might never see her again had been even harder to accept. However, because of my faith, I believed I would eventually see her again. Remaining in Crystal's life has been a great blessing. I'm sure there will be more blessings coming my way in my relationship with Crystal, and I am excited to be a part of it.

Two Gifts

When Crystal announced she was getting married, I thought it would be a great idea for my father Marshall, Robbie, and me to get breakfast together and then get tuxedos together since all three of us were going to be involved in the wedding. Three generations would be hanging out for the day. It was a great idea until I blew it.

We went to breakfast, but as soon as breakfast was over, my phone started ringing and instead of ignoring it for the day, as always, I felt I had to take every call. From the time we left the diner throughout the entire time we were getting fitted for the tuxedos, I was on the phone. About the time we were finished there, my father asked if we could take him home instead of going to lunch. On the way home, I continued to take calls. I dropped my father off, and Robbie and I headed home.

Within a couple of hours of taking my father home, I thought about the day and how rude I had been the entire time we were out. I called my father to apologize. When he answered the phone, I explained why I was calling, and when I finished talking, there was dead silence on the other line. "Dad! Dad!" I shouted. Still nothing on the other end of the line. Then suddenly I heard my mother's voice. She was asking me what I had said, but I wanted to know what happened to my father. She demanded to know again what I had said that could have upset my father. I told my mother I was calling to apologize to my dad for the way I acted. As my mother described it, when I finished apologizing, my father dropped the phone in tears and walked away.

My mother was able to get my father back on the phone after several minutes. I felt horrible at this point and couldn't stop apologizing to my dad. After a few seconds, he became speechless again. My mom grabbed the phone, and I told her that I was coming over to their house and we were going out to dinner. We went back and forth for a few minutes. My father said he didn't feel up to going out, but in my own stubbornness, I insisted I was coming over and I was going to make up for the way I had acted earlier.

A couple of hours later I had convinced my father to come to dinner at an Italian restaurant. My father and his siblings always made their own sausages—they weren't cooked, they were cured. It had been a family tradition for many years. To make the dinner with my parents a little more special, and to ensure my dad was in his element, I suggested he bring a "family sausage" to dinner. I knew the owner of the restaurant, and I knew he would allow us to include it with our meal. In the past, we had brought samples to the owner, and he sliced and shared the sausage with us over a glass of wine.

As dinner progressed, my dad loosened up and I could see how happy he was. He was an Italian immigrant, in an Italian restaurant, eating dinner and sharing stories with the owner as they spoke in Italian. I felt better at this point as I watched my dad enjoying himself.

After dinner, I took him to my daughter's indoor soccer game. He was in his element at dinner, and he was in his element now, as he watched the game he'd loved as a child. He was cheering the team on and smiling from ear to ear. At one point, I heard him sigh and mention how happy he was to be in this moment.

After the game, I took my parents home, and before bed, I reflected on the day's events. I considered the blessings of the day. My father had given me two gifts that day. The first was awareness—of how much he did care about spending time with Robbie and me. The second was the gift of humility. I hadn't thought it was important for him to spend time with me because, growing up, I *never* heard him express those feelings to me. Keep in mind, my dad was always working to support our family. I'm sure he would have wanted to spend more time with us, but he had to work for us to make it financially. Now as a parent, I understand parents' unspoken desires to spend time with their children. In my own ignorance and rudeness, I had underestimated how much it meant to my dad. His reaction was a gift I will never forget.

Prison Time

Approximately seven years ago, I accepted the opportunity to speak at a prison. I had been scheduled to speak for ninety minutes. *What was I going to talk to inmates about for ninety minutes?* I had fifteen to twenty years of personal growth and self-help experience, and I knew I could impact the inmates, but I couldn't decide what exactly I wanted to discuss—until I thought about my daughter Crystal.

I recalled a time in 2003 when I was at a seminar in Maui. My group engaged in a program activity called the "Journey Wall." The idea of the Journey Wall was to take a piece of paper and draw columns across the top of the page in five-year increments. I started my journey from the time I was fifteen years old. I wrote intervals from 15–20, 20–25, 25–30, and so on up to 50 years old. On the left side of the page we had rows going down the page in the following order: What happened? What was the victory? What was the lesson learned? Who played a part in it? Was the hand of Providence involved? We took roughly forty-five minutes to go through this activity.

In my case, for example, at age seventeen I became a dad. After two and a half years I was not able to see my daughter again for seven and a half years. We were reunited when I was twenty-seven. Other items I added to my Journey Wall included getting my license, my first job, and buying my first car, as well as negative things like getting into trouble here and there, losing $450,000, and what I learned from all these events.

I figured I could present this idea to the guys in prison to inspire them to believe that even though they were in prison as punishment, in time, something good could happen to them despite mistakes earlier in their lives.

I engaged in an interactive presentation with the inmates for the next ninety minutes. Showing up transparent for the guys, being authentic, allowed them to feel free to talk about their own mistakes. I believed when the guys could physically see their journey on paper and how a mistake could lead to a blessing, it would give them hope and something to look forward to. It was also a blessing to me to be able to share my story with these guys, and it was a gift to know they were impacted by the exercise. Sometimes you truly need to see it all on paper before you realize your life and the opportunities it holds for the future is better than you think.

There was something else to learn from this Journey Wall. When you look back at your journey, you will probably find some empty spaces. Your first thought may be to get down on yourself for not having an accomplishment in a given time frame. But the objective is to not have empty spaces going forward. Your awareness will be heightened by the simple fact that you will now be looking for your accomplishments, mistakes, lessons learned, and the people who were there for you along the way. You will find joy and fulfillment in what you discover!

REFLECTION QUESTIONS

- **Take some time to reflect on your life in five-year increments and go through this exercise. Allow yourself to be blessed by the awareness you receive from it.**
- **What have been your biggest wins in life?**
- **What are some of the lessons you have learned along the way?**
- **Who are the people that have been there for you?**
- **Do you feel the hand of Providence was involved?**

Blessing Others

Not only can we receive blessings, but we can *be* blessings to others. We can do this through our time, treasure, or talent. One way I try to live this is when we pass a homeless person on the street. My son and I will attend professional football and baseball games throughout the year, and inevitably while we are approaching the stadium, we encounter a homeless person. Thousands of fans pass by these homeless people at every event, never giving a thought to help. I know we can't help everyone, but I do know we can bless one person each time we go to an event. It has become such a habit between Robbie and me that we just look at each other and nod. He knows his job, and I know mine. I pull out a dollar or two, hand it to him, and he approaches the homeless person to hand him or her the money. Then he asks the question: What's your name?

While it's great to be able to give the money, it's even better to get a name. Here's why. As thousands of people pass the homeless every day, they don't acknowledge them. It's as if the man or woman is a fixture like a light pole or a post, not a human being. We are all human beings, and some of us have it better than others. I believe it's our God-given responsibility to help others in some way. It doesn't always have to be financially. It could be by offering a kind word, giving over a sandwich, or just by having a conversation. "Get a name," I say to Robbie every time. The moment we ask that person his name, he feels relevant. When we acknowledge another, we bless that individual. We always get a name and then say a prayer for the individual.

One little act of kindness could be all a person needs to make a change in his or her life. And each time we make this kind of connection, we in turn are blessed. What a powerful lesson to share with a child.

The next time you notice a homeless person, see the opportunity to bless someone and be blessed in return.

Blessings from Taking Our Own Advice

To be able to recognize blessings when they come your way is a gift in and of itself. I mention my children often, and that's because I am blessed to have the opportunity to learn more about them every day. In addition, I have been blessed with the opportunity to learn more about *me* through them. Watching Robbie and Amanda participate in several different sports over the years has shown me the many parallels between sports and life. I'm always coaching my kids in ways that allow them to see how what they learn on the court or in the field carries over into their lives. When I'm coaching my kids or other children, I sometimes make a comment that makes me wonder: *Did I just make that statement for them, or was I really talking to myself?*

One such moment occurred when I was thinking about Amanda and sports. When she plays soccer, basketball, or lacrosse, she sees the field very well. She's always looking to see her teammates' and their opponents' positions before shooting.

After every game, I talk to her about what she did well and what she could have done differently. She rolls her eyes quite frequently. My advice usually goes something like this:

"Amanda, you have to take your open shots."

"Don't be afraid to drive the lane."

"If the opportunity presents itself, you need to take advantage of it."

"Fake left, do a crossover dribble, then go right to the hoop. Either dish it off or take the shot."

Oftentimes, I receive responses from her that sound something like this:

"I don't want to look bad."

"I don't want to make a mistake."

"I don't want to look like a ball hog."

It never fails that every time we have this conversation,

I question whether I am talking to her or whether I am really talking to myself. I hear her answers as if they were responses to questions I ask myself.

Am I taking enough chances in my life and in my business to score? Do I see the business field well? If an opportunity presents itself to me, am I going to take advantage of it? If I am struggling to take my business to the next level, is it because I lack confidence or am I afraid to drive the lane and take the shot?

Would I reply with the same responses Amanda does? It's an interesting thought, and a question of self-awareness.

The answers to these questions are found in the questions themselves. If I'm having this kind of conversation with myself, then I know deep down I can be doing more. I know something within me—fear, perhaps, or appearing selfish, maybe—is preventing me from taking chances to do better.

At home after Amanda's last game, while we were having one of our usual discussions, I told her about this "a-ha moment." I let her know that after the next game, when I ask her these questions, she can answer first, and then she can fire right back at me with the same questions: *Dad, are you driving the lane? Dad, are you taking the shot when the opportunity presents itself?*

She smiled and said, "*Now I have something I can hold over your head.*" She then thanked me for sharing my struggle with her.

Just as I try to convey to Amanda—and to myself—there are times when you need to drive the lane, take the shot, or pass, I pose the same questions to you. Are you taking advantage of the opportunities that present themselves to you in your business and in life? If nothing external is holding you back and you're still not moving forward, you have to ask yourself what within you is keeping you from reaching the next level.

If it's fear, then it's time to recognize it, put it in a bottle, and leave it on a shelf. Then work through the steps to get where you want to be. You will find that the exercise frees you from boundaries you've created, and you may just end up being better to yourself and to the people around you.

I'm privileged to have coached my daughter and encourage her to continue moving forward despite her fears and insecurities. The awareness God has gifted me to recognize that I need to take my own advice is not only a blessing, but it is humbling as well. And if you can help others see things from this perspective when coaching, raising children, or leading a team in business, then that's a blessing too. The more open we are to living a learning-based life, the more our awareness increases, and this allows us to help others either directly or indirectly.

Reflect on your life and think about moments where you were trying to encourage others with some advice. Look deeper into the message you were attempting to share. Was it a message you were sharing for others or was it advice you needed to hear yourself? Then going forward, anytime you find yourself giving advice, make yourself aware of what's really going on in that moment and ask yourself the same question. As you continue to work on this, you will become more aware of it occurring in your life. It's an empowering exercise that will help you move forward in your life.

Teaching Moments

Blessings sometimes come in the form of teaching moments. Roughly ten years ago, Robbie and I were invited to accompany two friends to Las Vegas to attend the Monster Truck finals. Robbie had grown to love watching Monster Truck competition on television. He would watch the competition every morning before school. When we were asked to go, I saw it as an opportunity to do something with my son that I was sure he would remember for a lifetime.

We arrived in Vegas to an unbelievable amount of enthusiasm and excitement. I had no idea how big of a deal this was. As much of a non-fan as I was for this event, I couldn't help but get caught up in the excitement. The day prior to the show, there were all kinds of expos in the stadium parking lot. You could meet the drivers and get their autographs. We were able to buy t-shirts and model trucks. What caught my son's eye was a remote control (RC) car exhibition. Robbie was enamored by it. We stood and watched for at least an hour.

The show was an awesome experience. I was so happy to be able to spend this time with Robbie, but what I *didn't* know was the opportunity it would present in the coming weeks.

Within a week of coming home from the event, Robbie was online investigating where he could find these RC cars. He discovered there was a hobby shop ten minutes from our house and asked me to take him there.

We searched the store for a specific car, the Traxxas. It was amazing to both of us how many different types of RC cars existed—from battery-operated to gas-operated cars. Not only that, but there were so many different sizes as well. After about fifteen minutes or so, we finally found our car. Of course, the first thing that caught my eye was the price: $307. With a grin from ear to ear, Robbie looked at the car, then at me, and asked: "Can we buy it?"

I thought about it for what seemed like an eternity and then responded to Robbie gently, "You can't come down here, pick out a car at this price, and expect me to shell out $307. But I have an idea." I told him I had several customers who had to sell their homes. The homes were vacant, but the owners had to keep their lawns maintained. My idea was to call them and ask if Robbie and I could cut their grass until the houses sold. I explained why I was asking: (1) to teach Robbie the value of work, and (2) to enable Robbie to earn the money to buy his RC car. We would mow the lawns every other week, and my clients would write their checks for $25–$30 out to Robbie instead of me. When Robbie earned enough money, we would return to the hobby shop and purchase the car. Robbie wasn't crazy about the idea for a very simple reason: He wasn't getting his car that day.

After several weeks of cutting grass, my son had earned roughly $250. I told him it was time to get his car. "But Dad, I haven't earned enough money yet," he said. I told him he had proven to me his willingness to work hard for what he wanted, and I would give him the rest. Within a week's time, we went to the hobby shop to get his Traxxas. We pulled the car off the shelf, proceeded to the checkout line, and Robbie handed me this little sandwich bag with $250 inside.

I looked at him and responded, "This is your deal. You worked hard for this moment. I want you to make the exchange with the cashier so you can experience appreciation for the work you had to do to buy what you wanted." I gave him the remaining $57 he needed, and with a huge smile on his face, he turned to the cashier and gave her the $307 required to purchase his car.

Robbie and I were both blessed in this situation. I was blessed with the opportunity to teach my son the importance of working to earn money to buy what he desires. I could have certainly bought him the car and he would have been happy. If I had chosen that route, he would have learned *nothing* except to ask for what he wanted in the hope and expectation of getting it. He would have been disappointed had I said no from the beginning and not bought it at all. Instead, he was able to have skin in the game and earn the privilege to purchase his own RC car. Robbie was blessed with a valuable learning experience.

It was tough for me and my family growing up, but I consider it one of the many blessings God has given me. Were it not for the difficult journey and the work ethic instilled in me out of necessity, I would not have been able to give the life-lesson gift to Robbie. He understands the concept of working, and he appreciates the lesson taught.

More Blessed than We Realize

Blessings exist all around us. We only need to take the time to see them. Every evening before going to bed, I write in my journal for a few minutes. Several of the things I write about are amazing things that occurred during the day. Our days go by so fast, and sometimes we focus so much on the negatives or the stresses of the day that we fail to see all the blessings.

Blessings occur all around us every day. Be willing to see the blessing in everything and every moment. You will live a much richer and fuller life if you choose to keep your mind open to what's going on around you.

I began this chapter talking about my favorite answer I like to hear from people when asked how they're doing: "I'm blessed." I finish this chapter by telling you how blessed I am to have reflected on all the goodness in my life and all the experiences I have been able to have and to truly see them as gifts from God.

REFLECTION QUESTIONS

- **How have you been blessed in your life?**
- **What perceived negative experiences have you had in your life that in reality were blessings?**
- **Who have you been a blessing to, and who can you bless today, tomorrow, and in the months and years to come?**

CHAPTER 12

RECOGNIZING
THE ABUNDANCE EVERYWHERE

HAVE YOU TAKEN the time to reflect and understand how much abundance exists all around you? Is there abundance in the air you breathe? The people you see? The penny you find on the street? The stars you see in the night sky? Abundance is everywhere! You only need to be aware that it exists.

Abundance Leads to More

One of my favorite examples of abundance is how a home garden produces its fruits and vegetables. I started gardening four years ago. My first attempt proved satisfactory but wasn't what I had expected. We had bought our house brand new twelve years ago, and if you know anything about new construction, you know that when the developer comes in to clear the land, they usually skim all the good soil off the top, leaving only a clay foundation. After the houses are built, sod is laid directly on top of the clay, leaving no good soil to plant a vegetable garden.

When I started four years ago, I cleared a section of my yard and planted peppers, zucchini, eggplant, tomatoes, and more. At season's end, I harvested a decent crop, but nowhere what I imagined. What I learned was obvious—my vegetables didn't have enough good soil for nourishment. Instead of a rich soil, the roots were trying to grow in a hard clay. I decided the next year I would build garden boxes.

I built three large garden boxes, each twenty inches in depth, so I could fill them with plenty of soil and allow the roots of the plants to grow. I scraped what little soil layered the clay and pushed it aside to mix in later. Our county dump has some of the best compost in the state, of which I added a substantial amount plus three hundred pounds of horse manure and a couple bags of Miracle-Gro soil. Then I added back the original soil and tilled it all together. My garden was ready for seeding!

Within weeks my garden was exploding with plants. I had tomato plants, peppers, eggplant, cucumbers, and more. My zucchini plants were huge! My neighbor came over one day and asked what I was doing to create such abundance. He had never seen zucchini leaves that big before. The tomato plants had grown to over seven feet tall. It was amazing! I had a thriving garden, and I knew I was going to enjoy an impressive crop.

A few weeks later, the garden started to bear fruit. As I harvested some of the vegetables, I thought about farming in general and wondered how anyone could go hungry in this country. God gives us this beautiful earth, and He even says in the Bible that He will look after the tiniest sparrows of the world. Abundance is all around us, but we don't take the time to see it.

I decided to jar banana peppers that summer. There were sixty to seventy banana peppers lying on my counter as I prepared to jar them. First, I needed to cut the top off each pepper and clean out all the seeds. As I cut open pepper after pepper and saw how many seeds were in one pepper, I was amazed at how much one seed can produce.

One seed produces a plant, and from each plant grows thirty to forty peppers. Within each pepper there must have been at least one hundred seeds, which, if planted, could produce another one hundred plants producing another thirty to forty peppers per plant. Keep multiplying that by one hundred seeds per plant and the numbers are astounding.

Sociologists say each person knows, on average, 275 people. For each person I connect deeply with, that means I have access to the 275 people they know. Do the math—for every ten people I connect with on a deeper level, that's 2,750 people I can meet, and on and on. There is an abundance of relationships to create out there and to lose sight of that is to think in scarcity. There will be relationships that do not last long and there will be some that do not go well, but as long as you continue to cast your net, you will obtain new opportunities.

Many similarities exist between building a business database and planting a bountiful garden. Pruning the plants in your garden allows them to produce more. You also have to prune your database. You have to continually sort and qualify a database, and it will produce more. If a relationship is not producing the fruit you would like to see, then you must move on and focus on the ones that *are* producing. More will come from that.

Abundance versus Scarcity

Abundance comes in many ways, but you have to believe it's there if you really expect to see it. The opposite of abundance is scarcity. I grew up in a family of seven siblings. We struggled financially and didn't have much. I was competitive in every sense of the word, and if I had something, I didn't want to give it up or share it because I didn't believe there was enough to go around. I believed if someone were to accumulate wealth, then someone else would have to be poor. That is a zero-sum, or scarcity, mindset.

When I first got into my business of selling real estate, I had a mindset that if someone won a listing, then I actually *lost* the listing. It's a view that there's not enough to go around. But if you believe there is more than enough to go around and are willing to share your thoughts and ideas, then you have an *abundant mindset*. Most real estate agents wouldn't dare share an idea or thought of how to gain more clients because they believe competitiveness means benefiting off scarcity. But I believe in the idea of sharing— because now I do believe there is enough for everyone.

To think abundantly or in terms of scarcity is a choice. If you think in scarcity, you may live in poverty or may constantly struggle. When you choose to think abundantly, your world changes. You will see life in a different way that allows you to be able to give more freely.

Less Is More

Just being a giver indicates you have an abundant mindset. People generally do not give because they feel when they do, they will have less of something. But the opposite is true. The more we give, the more we receive. It's a cliché, but it is truth. Call it karma; call it the Universe. I choose to call it God working on our behalf; the more we give, the more God works on our behalf to give us more. Essentially, letting go of or giving away something opens us up to receive more.

A good example of this, in my experience, is in the practice of Contemplative Prayer. The idea, as I explained earlier in this book, is to clear your mind of your thoughts. When we detach ourselves from thoughts via prayer, we open our minds to receive more clarity in our lives. For years I have practiced Contemplative Prayer, and what I know is this: Spending fifteen to twenty minutes a day in Contemplative Prayer has helped me see more clearly. It has also given me more peace of mind. And it has enabled me to release my hold on scarcity thinking.

When I go to an appointment to list a house for sale, I explain to my clients the concept of *less is more*. I explain this from a buyer's point of view; buyers look for space in a home. To create space, the seller has to remove things. I explain to my clients that less on the walls, on the floors, and on the countertops means more space. Again, to have less of one thing means you have more of another. You have fewer objects, but you have an abundance of space.

Another way to create more in our lives is to eliminate the unnecessary elements. I look at my schedule every week, and I am a guy who feels the need to be busy all the time. This, in some concocted way, makes me feel good. But what I have discovered is the fuller my schedule, the more stressed I become. How often do you find yourself scheduling unnecessary appointments during your week?

BETTER THAN YOU THINK

By eliminating unnecessary appointments in my week, I create more time to do what is important for my business and my life. Less is truly more. I can be more present in the moment and less stressed. I will find an abundance of peace and energy. People don't realize how much energy is lost in worrying about how to get tasks accomplished or completed.

Counterintuitively, saying "no" is another way to create abundance in our lives. I once heard years ago that successful people say "yes" all the time and just figure things out. So, I decided if I wanted to be successful, I needed to be a "yes" man. But by doing that I couldn't always find a way to make things work. I was stressed and anxious all the time. I asked myself, *How can I say "no" or turn someone down after I've already said "yes"*? I became a "yes" man and a "people pleaser." All this did was create more stress in my life, which affected other areas of my life.

I wish I could say I'm an expert at saying "no," but I'm not. I am, however, getting better at it. Learning to say "no" creates opportunities to say "yes" to the more important things and people in my life. "No" creates abundance for me. It creates an abundance of not just more time in my life, but more peace.

A State of Awe

I love driving on the highway in an area where there are thousands of trees surrounding me in early spring just before the leaves start to blossom. It seems sometimes I'll be driving and see nothing but bare trees, and then a few days later, or sometimes even the next day, the trees are covered with leaves. It's a beautiful sight and a beautiful thought. One moment there is nothing, and then suddenly there is an abundance of leaves on the trees.

That's how life is, and that is how abundance can show up in our lives. One moment we feel this emptiness or nothingness, and suddenly God blesses us with abundance. You have to be aware that it exists, you have to believe it's coming your way, and you have to accept it when it arrives. Without being aware of the abundance around you, you won't be able to experience it when it shows up. You know the trees are going to blossom; you just don't know exactly when. In life, if you believe abundance will come your way, it will, but you won't know exactly *when*. That doesn't matter as long as you are in alignment with good values and principles. When we are out of alignment or not acting in accordance with our values, we can create anxiety in our lives, thus shutting down our ability to be aware of the abundance that exists all around us.

Love, Knowledge, Wisdom, and Courage

How about having an abundance of love, knowledge, wisdom, and courage? There doesn't ever have to be an end to the amount of love you can give to your spouse, children, those around you, or even strangers. God never said *you only have so much love to give from your tank, and once it's used up, there is no more.* He never suggested there was only so much wisdom or knowledge we could gain in our lifetime or a limit to how much we could share with others. I don't think God ever said *there is only so much courage you can have, so be careful what you attempt to do in life because once you go through this supply of courage, there won't be any left to use in another situation.* There is an endless supply of love, knowledge, wisdom, and courage. Abundance exists everywhere in our lives; we only have to take the time to see it and allow ourselves to experience it.

We gain wisdom and knowledge from the books we read, our experiences, the mistakes we make, and the people we meet. There are endless ways to gain wisdom and knowledge. For example, King Solomon never asked for the material things in life; he asked God for wisdom and knowledge. God granted his request, which eventually allowed him to become the richest man of his era. There is no shortage of wisdom and knowledge.

The same can be said for courage and love. Can you ever love your spouse and children too much? Could you ever say to yourself, *I used up all the courage I have, and because of that I can never try anything new again in my life?* The answer to these questions is No! Why? Because there is an abundant, never-ending supply.

Can there be an end to the amount of knowledge, wisdom, love, courage, and confidence we can receive? No! Then why would we put a limitation on who and what we can be? God wants us to have abundance and fullness in our lives. He is willing to give it to us in avalanches if we allow it.

Letting Go

If we would only take the time to see all there is to see in this world, we would know how much is available to us. If we choose to see the world from a scarcity mindset, then we come from a place of harsh competition. However, if we see the world from an abundance mindset, we come from a mindset of creation. The world is always creating on our behalf. They say the universe is always expanding. Think about the cells in our bodies. They are always regenerating. Abundance exists everywhere!

When we take the time to appreciate and be grateful for all we already have in our lives, we will see more come our way. This is especially true when we decide to let go of things and thoughts. The word I like to use here is "detachment." When we become too attached to things and thoughts in our lives, we are blocking and preventing new ideas and experiences from entering our lives. The key is to let go, to detach from objects cluttering our lives and thoughts cluttering our minds.

When we train ourselves to let go, we create an environment of magnanimity. If we all took the time to reflect about what's important in our lives, we would choose fulfillment, freedom, and peace. The highest of the three is peace. We can't have peace if we're not fulfilled, and we can't have peace if we don't feel free. Detachment leads to freedom and fulfillment, which ultimately lead to peace.

To detach from something means not to put too much value in something or someone. For instance, if we constantly avoid doing things or making decisions in fear of what others think, then we are attached to that worry. If we constantly worry about something, we use up energy that we could spend elsewhere for a better purpose. However, if we detach ourselves from those worries, we are free to allow better thoughts and ideas into our minds. That's a challenging task. There is an abundance of peace waiting for us if we allow ourselves the opportunity to achieve it.

When was the last time you purposefully stopped what you were doing and thought about all you already have in your life?

When was the last time you thanked God for all the blessings you've received? The next time you get anxious about your future or about what you *don't* have—Stop! Stop yourself right where you are in the moment and be grateful for what you have, where you are, and most importantly, who you are. The better we can get at being aware of this, the more peace and fulfillment we will discover in our lives.

REFLECTION QUESTIONS

- What is your state of thinking?
- Is it one of abundance or scarcity?
- Do you believe in the concept of "less is more?" If so, how has it shown up in your life?
- Where in your life could you remove things in order to have more?
- What causes you to be in a state of awe?

CHAPTER **13**

THE MAGIC
OF GRATITUDE

WHEN WE WERE YOUNG, we were taught two important words—*please* and *thank you.* When we are thankful for something, we are showing how appreciative we are.

We are grateful for acts of kindness directed our way, for a safe trip, for the food we eat, when someone we love recovers from an injury or surgery, and we are most grateful when we or someone we know survives a potential tragedy. There is so much to be thankful for in our everyday lives as well. There are things happening around us all the time that we take for granted. The tendency in our society is to be grateful only for the good things that come our way. Put in a different perspective, how often do we give thanks for our challenges or our struggles?

Exercises in Gratitude

I have always thought of myself as being grateful for everything and have taught my children to do the same. I learned this in part from the book *The Magic* by Rhonda Byrne. It helped me see things in a different way. *The Magic* is a book designed to increase our awareness of all there is to be thankful for. You could actually look at it as a workbook. For twenty-eight consecutive days, you are expected to write ten things you're grateful for in addition to completing other daily tasks. At the end of twenty-eight days, you have 280 different things, people, items, situations, and so on to be grateful for.

One of the exercises required me to start the day by saying thank you for the great news I was going to receive that day. Right away my radar was on high alert waiting for some *great news* to come *my* way.

Prior to reading the book, I had been hired for a speaking presentation for a region of Wells Fargo's loan officers in Maryland. The presentation went extremely well, and, in fact, the manager at the time called me to thank me and said he would be referring me to other regional managers for another opportunity to speak.

I had gone through most of the day and nothing stood out as *great news* yet. I wrapped up my final appointment at 9:30 p.m. and still nothing. When I returned home, I checked my voice mail. I had a message from a regional manager of Wells Fargo in northern Virginia. He wanted me to speak to his regional loan officers and offered me a fee. That was my *great news* and what I had been waiting for! I couldn't believe this program was actually working.

Another part of the exercise requires you to name a mistake you have made and pick ten things you are thankful for as a result of the mistake. This really helps us to accept failure as a path to learning and is a powerful tool for understanding how your life can be better than you think, even in a moment that feels difficult.

So many of us will not do something for fear of failing, or when we *do* fail, we do not see the blessings beyond the failure. When I wrote out my mistake and discovered the good things that had come from that mistake, I was counting my blessings.

The exercises in *The Magic* are *truly* all about awareness. They not only increase your awareness of all you have to be grateful for, but they also allow you to see where you are on your journey and how much gratitude you truly possess.

Without going through the entire list of twenty-eight exercises, I can tell you wholeheartedly that there are multiple ways and areas of our lives where we can be grateful if we open our eyes, our minds, and our hearts.

Sharing in Others' Good Fortune

I reread the book the following year with the idea of doing the exercises more purposefully and actually feeling the gratitude in my heart when I said thank you.

Two weeks into the second reading of the book, I came upon the same assignment—being grateful for the *great news* I was going to receive that day. I was going about my day like the last time, expecting to hear great news for me and about me. It was two o'clock on a Sunday afternoon, and nothing had come my way yet. Then my phone rang. It was my mother calling. "Rob," she said, "I was calling to give you some *great news* that was just delivered to us." I smiled from ear to ear. My mother continued on. "Your father and I received a letter in the mail yesterday—from the bank. It said we had officially paid the mortgage in full on our house." That was, of course, *great news*! My initial thinking was such that the great news was supposed to be about me and for me. As I reflected in that split second, it hit me: *Yes, this was the great news.* This was unbelievable news! My parents had bought their first house in 1967 and now, forty-nine years later, they finally owned a house of their own. Wow!

After hanging up the phone, I smiled and thought about what I had read that morning regarding great news. This really made me contemplate where I was on my journey of my own personal growth. Yes, *The Magic* was about gratitude and how it changes not only our lives, but also the lives of others. This humbling lesson helped me to see the importance of being happy for others and being thankful for the great news they receive. It also taught me to be happy for others' good fortune.

Finding Gratitude in My Impatience

Another exercise in the book had me being grateful for all the service providers in my life. I am in a sales business, working with several service providers daily. I have occasionally been impatient, causing me to be short and somewhat disrespectful to the service providers over the phone.

One evening, on a cold windy night in January, I was trying to change out a lockbox on one of my sales listings. It was about twenty degrees, but it felt like ten degrees with the wind blowing. I had no hat, no gloves, and only a light jacket on. The lockbox was not working properly, so I called the service department. There is an entire protocol I must perform before I can determine the exact problem or whether the lockbox should be declared defective. I was patient at first, and on more than one occasion I let the girl on the line know how cold it was and asked if she could speed the process up a bit. She was doing all she could. I suspected the motor was not working correctly. But she said it was the battery, not the motor. Every signal I received throughout the process was strong, leading me to believe it was not the battery, but she was in control and there was nothing I could do. I started raising my voice in displeasure. At this point, there was nothing I could do except come back with bolt cutters, cut the lock off, and then break open the lockbox so I could retrieve the key.

As I pulled away from the house, I was thinking about the book and how I had treated the woman on the phone. During the process, I kept telling myself to be grateful, but it was so cold and it was taking way too long to fix the problem. I lost my patience. I felt extremely bad for how I treated her and the awareness of it all humbled me. This process of gratitude is not only about being grateful to receive things; it's also about gaining an understanding of where you are on your own journey. I have a long way to go and so much more to be thankful for. I didn't get the lock open, and I wasted some time. What I did receive was a huge blessing, a lesson in humility. Gratitude prepares us for blessings. We tend to believe a blessing is a receipt of something positive. But how we define "positive" is relative. On the surface, my phone exchange may seem like a negative, but the gift was the awareness of how I had treated her and how I had been treating others when I was not getting my way. Becoming aware of this pattern of reaction allowed me to work harder to stop repeating it.

The Snowstorm

A record 29.2 inches of snow fell in the Baltimore area over a twenty-nine-hour period in 2016. Not only were several inches of snow predicted for the area, but high winds were also expected. With the pending storm coming, my son and I conceived a plan to attack the snow twice over its duration so we would not have to shovel the entire amount at one time. We had seven customers' houses to shovel. Because it had been about a year since we last used the snowblower, we tested it out Thursday evening to be sure it was running okay. The snow began Friday afternoon and was expected to last through Saturday evening. We decided we would go out on our first run Saturday morning and do our second run Sunday morning.

Twelve to fifteen inches of snow had fallen when we began. It was heavy, and the wind was blowing hard. As we were about halfway through the sixth house, I noticed the blower was struggling to run. It continued to worsen as we began the seventh house. To keep the blower running, I had to run it in the choke mode the rest of the way. Because of that, it took longer to clear the snow. Robbie and I finished the day knowing we would have to come back and do this all over again the next morning.

My assignment the next day from *The Magic* was to think about three things I was struggling with and write them down. Then in a sentence, I was to write *thank you for the magnificent outcome for* _____. The one obvious magnificent outcome I was hoping for was not only for the snowblower to start, but for it to run at full speed. Running at full speed, we could finish all the houses we had started the day before with no problem.

Robbie and I got bundled up and prepared for the cold, the wind, and the snow that awaited us outside. We opened the garage door, pushed the snowblower in the path we had shoveled outside the door, primed the motor, and pulled the cord. To my delight, the blower started immediately. We were in business, and we were going to have a magnificent day!

We knocked out the first two houses in no time and then hit the third. We were about two-thirds through the third house when the snowblower suddenly shut off. *How could this be?* I checked the gas and the manual and could find nothing wrong. After a little break, I primed it again, pulled the cord, and bang, we were back in business. We finished the fourth and fifth houses with no problems. We were two-thirds through the sixth house when I noticed the snowblower beginning to struggle again. We finished the sixth house and moved on to the last house. Things were going well until we had about fifteen minutes' worth of work left. Unfortunately, I let the snowblower run out of gas! Big mistake! I filled the tank with gas and then pulled the cord to start the engine. That's when the day started to go crazy.

When I pulled the cord after refilling, the entire cord came out of the casing. I was in shock, not to mention there remained a huge pile of snow blocking the driveway we would have to dig through by hand. We had made it this far, and there was no sense in complaining. We were spared when a neighbor across the street snowblowing his walk and driveway cleared the rest of our snow in five minutes. Finished, we headed home. I had to push the blower through the street—not totally plowed yet—and through other areas of the neighborhood clogged with twenty-five-plus inches of snow, and finally, up a small hill to our house.

Once there, I was exhausted, but we still had a section of our own driveway to dig through.

A neighbor up the street fixed the broken pull-cord in thirty minutes. I reattached the casing and proceeded to crank up the engine. This time when I pulled the cord, it broke from the handle and the cord recoiled back into the casing. I could only laugh at this point. Murphy's Law was well in play here! I immediately went back to my neighbor, and within ten minutes he had come to the rescue yet again. We attached the casing back to the blower, cranked it up again, and we were back in business!

Up until this point, our street had not been plowed, but as we anticipated, the county truck's eventual passage pushed huge amounts of snow back in front of everyone's recently cleared driveways. It was time to go to work for what we hoped would be the last time for this storm.

I started my blower up again, and along with two other neighbors and their blowers, and three other people, including my son, we went on to clear about eight neighbors' driveways. Within a few minutes a bolt came loose and fell out of my blower, which hindered the steering. The cord that allowed the wheels to spin got so loose; the blower lost its self-propelling capability. I could only shake my head in disbelief. We were able to tighten the cord, worked through the missing bolt issue, and were finished by 8:00 p.m.

After the last house, we headed up the small hill to our garage with a very banged-up blower that had been through thirteen plus hours of snowblowing. Just when I gave it its last push to its resting spot, the shift lever snapped. All I could do was laugh. The end of a magnificent day!

Let's examine the gratitude I was *supposed* to have for the magnificent outcome. *Thank you for the magnificent outcome today! Nothing* in that statement says anything at all about the journey. It speaks specifically to the *outcome.* The outcome was such that we were able to clear all the walks we set out to clear and my son made good money that day. There was also gratitude in the journey. I started the day worrying if the snowblower was even going to start. It did! Then I was worried if it would last long enough for us to clear all the walks we had committed to clearing. It did that as well.

When the snowblower broke down the first time, a neighbor offered to help us finish clearing the walk we were working on. An awesome experience through the day's journey—someone who was in the middle of clearing his own walk of twenty-nine inches of snow stopped to help us finish ours. Amazing! Then when our cord broke—twice—another neighbor helped fix that problem both times. Incredible! When the county plow got stuck on our street, several neighbors worked to dig him out instead of yelling and screaming at the driver. Crazy! Finally, when the plow came through for the last time, three guys with snowblowers and another three or four people with shovels all pitched in, and in a very short period of time, helped clear as many as eight driveway aprons of our neighbors. Another thing to keep in mind is the sense of community created among neighbors when this happened.

Gratitude helps you put things in perspective. It provides the skills of looking at things from a different angle and finding the positive aspect of any event. When you consistently come from a place of gratitude, your heart softens in a good way. You live and work from a place of peace and unselfishness.

REFLECTION QUESTIONS

- **What exercise of gratitude do you practice consistently?**
- **Can you think of a time when you shared in another's good fortune? What happened?**
- **What magnificent things have occurred in your life?**
- **Are you purposeful about seeing magnificent outcomes on a daily basis in your life? How so?**
- **If you don't have a practice currently, what could you start doing daily to help you better see the blessings in your life?**

The Little Things

It says in the Bible, "Be faithful with little and you'll be given plenty." What does this mean? It means be grateful for the little things in life and you are bound to receive abundance.

Often, we show gratitude when momentous beneficial things happen to us. We express gratitude when we heal from an injury or sickness. If we win an award, we may give thanks in a speech. If you manage a major deal and receive a significant compensation for it, you give thanks for that. It's traditional for families to say grace before Thanksgiving dinner, but do we also give thanks for every meal?

Are we grateful for the simple and small things in our lives? Have you ever seen a penny lying on the ground and decided not to pick it up in fear of what someone may think or say about you? Years ago, I saw a penny lying on the floor in the locker room of a gym I attended. I looked around to make sure no one saw me picking it up before I took it. I was insecure about what anyone might think of me for picking it up. Out of nowhere the thought struck me, *Am I grateful for the little things in life?* I bent over, picked up the penny, and said to myself, *Lord, thank you for the abundance you sent my way today.* Since then, whenever I see a penny, nickel, or any change lying on the ground, I enthusiastically bend over, pick it up, and whisper, *Lord thank you for the abundance you sent my way today.*

One day my wife and I were in our car, and I was telling her about this new habit I had about being grateful every time I found money on the street. As I was finishing my story, we pulled into a gas station. I exited my car, started pumping the gas, and looked down to find a quarter lying at my feet. I picked up the quarter, offered my thanks to God for the abundance, and then smiled in amazement of what had just transpired. I opened the car door, looked at Debbie, and said, "Can you believe this? We just finished talking about this, and look what I found." I smiled again and flipped the quarter to her.

We left the gas station and drove to J.C. Penny's. We picked up whatever it was we went there to purchase and proceeded to the checkout counter. As Debbie approached the counter, I looked down to my left and saw two quarters lying on the ground next to me. I couldn't help but laugh. Within a very short time period of showing my gratitude for the pennies, I was gifted three quarters. What an amazing chain of events had occurred there!

If we show gratitude and appreciation for such little things in life, then God will present bigger opportunities for us.

Be Grateful for What You Have

Many times in life I have become frustrated about what I *don't* have in my life. It might be things such as not achieving enough success, or not making enough money, or not having as much time with my family as I would like. This is not a good perspective. If I'm not grateful for what I have, how can I expect to have more?

In my real estate business, I host a quarterly Business Mixer, a networking event to which I invite anyone in my database who is a business owner or a salesperson. I remember how anxious I was about my first mixer. I had no model to follow and knew no one who had tried it previously whom I could ask for advice. My objective was to bring a bunch of people together in hopes of helping them to connect and exchange referrals. Even if I couldn't give someone a direct referral, I hoped my invitees could find value in the networking opportunity and become referral partners themselves.

I had no idea what to expect the first time I hosted my mixer event. Forty-one people attended! I deemed it a huge success. That would be the most people to attend for almost ten years. I believed the event was failing. The mistake I was making was to define my own self-worth and success on the number of people in attendance. I struggled with this notion for several years as the

THE MAGIC OF GRATITUDE

attendance dwindled from event to event. When my lowest attendance reached twelve, I called my business coach up to tell her, "I don't know if I want to have these events any longer." She encouraged me to continue with the events and to invest my time and energy in those who showed up.

What I learned was to be thankful for whoever attended and not worry about those who didn't. I needed to engage those who attended and give them my all. If my goal in life is to have an impact on people, it doesn't have to be in mass quantities. It can be one person at a time if that is what is supposed to happen. It took me back to the Biblical quote, "Be thankful for a little and you'll be given much." If I can't be thankful for what I have, why do I think I deserve more? I don't.

REFLECTION QUESTIONS

- **Think back to a time or an event where you got so caught up in what you didn't have or who wasn't present for a party, and consider these questions:**
- **If you had focused more on what you did have or who was there, how might the experience have been different for you?**
- **Were you really present in the moment?**
- **Were you grateful for what you had, or did you spend too much time complaining about what you didn't have?**

Gratitude for Time

What about the intangible things in life? Are we grateful for those as well? In his book *The Five Love Languages*, Gary Chapman shares with us how to better communicate with others by understanding our own love language. When we are able to do this, we can better understand how others need to be loved. The five love languages are Words of Affirmation, Physical Touch, Time, Acts of Service, and Gifts. Of the five, I think the most underappreciated of all of them is Time.

I read the book years ago, and my love language is Words of Affirmation. In the process of discovering my love language, I obviously thought it was important to also understand my wife's. Debbie's love language is Time. In our relationship, Debbie only needs me to be close by for her to feel loved, and when that happens, she is grateful. Our children ask frequently, "What time will you be home from work tonight?" They don't always ask because they want to do something when I get home. They only want me to *be home*. They want my *time*, and when I am home and spend time with them, my children not only feel loved, but they are also grateful for the time I have with them.

We all take time for granted. Society tends to take time for granted and believes we always have enough. However, our time is limited and it's precious so we must make the most of each moment in time because when our time on earth ends, will we be able to look back and be thankful for the time we had and the time we spent with the people we loved? Or are we going to look back and see how much time we wasted doing unnecessary things that had no importance in our lives? Time is our most precious

THE MAGIC OF GRATITUDE

commodity. Why waste a single minute? Be grateful for every minute you have in your life and spend your time wisely.

The Journey

Too often, we think ahead about achieving and accumulating more in our lives. We may get frustrated when we don't achieve our goals. Instead of getting frustrated, it's important to reflect on the journey and appreciate the process of trying to accomplish your goal—be grateful for that.

There will be struggles, hardships, and obstacles along the journey. I experienced an incredible journey with my goal to play professional baseball. Was I disappointed I didn't make it to the major leagues? Yes! But I was even more grateful for the experiences God allowed me along the journey from playing little league baseball to finishing my baseball career at FAU.

Yes, those were challenging days growing up the way we did, and others have had it tougher. I wouldn't want my children to have to struggle the way we did, but given the opportunity to do it again and knowing who I would become as a person because of that, I would most definitely do it again.

I'm so grateful for my life and how I grew up. I appreciate what my parents did for us and how they taught us. Blessings are what we receive when we are grateful for a challenge. There is not a single person who hasn't experienced some kind of challenge or impediment in his or her life. For the most part, people will attempt to go around them, over them, under them, and do everything in their power to avoid them. Why? We see a challenge as a source of pain or suffering. When we wrap our arms around an impediment or an obstacle in our lives and say *thank you* for that opportunity, good things are bound to happen.

Think back to struggles or challenges you have endured over the years, and consider where those challenges have led you. Do you think those experiences—no matter how hard they seemed to be—were actually bad experiences? At the time you may have thought, *There is no way I want to go through that again.* But look where you are now and who you have become. Would you be here and be that person if not for the difficult experiences? The best thing you can do is to be grateful for the journey.

There are some days when I question my success. When I look down that road, I have to stop myself and count my blessings. I have a good life. I have been blessed with a beautiful wife, three awesome children, and a precious granddaughter. I have been extremely successful in my business, and I have built many great relationships locally and across the country. My family and I are healthy, and we live a simple life. I have a strong faith, and God has blessed me with an awareness to see all the good He has granted me, and for that I am sincerely grateful.

Sincere gratitude opens the door to receive more and to be more. To have sincere gratitude means to feel the appreciation in your heart when you give your thanks and not to say a meaningless *thank you*.

Gratitude Is a Choice

We have a choice to express our gratitude every day. When things are going great or even when they are not going so well, we can choose to be grateful. We can whine and fuss about all the negatives or we can find gratitude in the positives from the experience.

Choosing gratitude is so easy, yet so hard for many of us. Gratitude is the foundation by which all good things come to pass. Are you aware of all that you could be more grateful for in your life? Show me a person who is sincerely grateful, and I will show you a person who has good things going on in his or her life and a person who feels fulfilled. I will also show you a person who lives in peace and harmony.

REFLECTION QUESTIONS

- **How can you show more gratitude for time?**
- **Write a list of some of your biggest challenges in your life. What about those challenges could you express gratitude for?**
- **How have you made gratitude a choice in your life?**

CHAPTER 14

UNCONDITIONAL LOVE FREES YOU

YOU OFTEN HEAR people speak of unconditional love. What does that really mean? Merriam-Webster defines it as: *to love without limitations or conditions.* Having an awareness of unconditional love and understanding it and then learning how to love unconditionally can lead to a fulfilling life. But how hard is it to love unconditionally? Extremely hard!

To love unconditionally is easier said than done because we live in a world brimming with judgment, resentment, grudges, and blame. You've heard the expression "forgive and forget." It is far easier to forgive than to forget, and we know how tough it is to forgive someone when we've been seriously wronged. How do we program ourselves to love without conditions?

The greatest example of unconditional love is the one set forth by Jesus Christ over 2000 years ago. Christ bore the weight of all our sins when crucified. As He suffered through the passion to be tortured, whipped, and nailed to the cross, He continued to love us. Even as He was hanging on the cross dying for our sins,

He uttered the words, "Father, forgive them, for they know not what they do." To me, this constitutes the ultimate demonstration of unconditional love.

As I continue to live my Catholic faith, I am more exposed to His unconditional love every day. I have made plenty of mistakes in my life, yet I know and believe, no matter what, God loves me and will continue to love me in both my darkest and brightest of times. Once I mentioned to a priest that I was speechless at the thought of God loving me even at my lowest of times. His response: "Rob, it is said that when you experience God's unconditional love, you should be left speechless."

God loves us always and forever, no matter who we are or what we have done in our lives. He gave us free will, which allows us to fall. God never leaves us. If we feel He is not a part of our lives, it's because we have made the choice to move away from Him.

The Prodigal Son

A great biblical story of unconditional love is that of the prodigal son (Luke 15:11–32). It depicts a wealthy father who has two sons. One of the sons, eager to experience life on his own, asks for his inheritance early and leaves his family. Within a very short time, he squanders all his money and is left with nothing. Shortly thereafter, a famine strikes, and the boy must hire himself out. He is sent to a field to feed pigs. The young man is so hungry that he is relegated to eating the pods he is supposed to feed to the pigs. One day, coming to his senses, he realizes what he has lost and what he has left behind. He decides to return home.

As the boy approaches from a distance, his father sees him. His father drops everything and runs to meet his son in the open fields and welcomes him with open arms. His father orders his people to slaughter the best calf and prepare for a celebration.

The father could have certainly been bitter and held a grudge against his son, but instead he welcomed and loved him like never before. The boy's father had no conditions upon which to celebrate the return of his son but rejoiced regardless of what had happened in the past. Unconditional love bears no grudges; it just is.

In this story we must understand that God is the Father and the son represents us. How often do we sin or turn our backs on God? No matter how grave the sin, God always welcomes us back and He celebrates our return to Him with no conditions. In our lives we can play the role of either the father or the son. You may be the parent whose child turns his back on you, or you may have been the child who turned your back on your parents. In either case, you have the opportunity to give or receive love unconditionally.

Our Family

I think of not only receiving unconditional love from God, but also from my spouse, children, friends, clients, and even strangers. On numerous occasions as a dad, I have lost patience with my children. I may have had a challenging day at work and when I came home, I would take out my frustrations on them. I would be short with them, or if they did something small I didn't approve of, I would yell at them. Then, realizing I was wrong, I would apologize. My kids would always say, "It's okay, Dad." Looking back, I am so grateful for the gift of unconditional love my children blessed me with. They could have easily shut down and pulled away from me, but instead, they welcomed me back with open arms. Children can be the most forgiving individuals. God says we should be like the children of this world.

My wife has been tolerating my crazy schedule for years. She always finds it in her heart to love me for what is. We have had our challenging moments, as any couple has, but she is always there for me. Despite some difficulties, she has never stopped loving me. I think one of the blessings of unconditional love is this: Once you receive it, you also want to give it out.

Forgiveness and the Burden of Not Forgiving

Forgiveness is a foundational piece of unconditional love. You've heard the phrase, "Love others the way you want to be loved." When we forgive, we are expressing our unconditional love. Have you ever had a close friend for years and then the relationship went sideways? You've gone from best of friends to not even speaking to one another. As I mentioned earlier, I experienced this years ago. Even though our friendship went sour, that friend remains a big part of my story, and I will always be grateful for the season of our friendship. If by some chance there arose an opportunity for our friendship to be reconciled, I would welcome it with no conditions.

When someone has wronged you, it's easy to hold a grudge; however, in doing so you carry a burden in your heart. This burden is like a poison that works its way through your body. The longer you hold onto the grudge, the harder it is to release the poison. As you continue to hold on to the poison, it will make you toxic without you even noticing it. The toxicity is not only in your mind; it can manifest itself in your behavior. While holding on to the grudge, you may be short-tempered with others. You may not forgive others as easily. You won't have the focus in your life to do the things you may want to accomplish or be the person you need to be because the poison boils up inside and consumes you. Once you allow yourself to forgive with no conditions, you allow yourself to be free.

REFLECTION QUESTIONS

- **Was there a time in your life when you acted like the prodigal son? Explain.**
- **Was there ever a time in your life where you wronged someone and that person struggled to forgive you? If so, how did it make you feel not to be forgiven? If and when you were forgiven, how did you feel?**

A Parent's Unconditional Love

If you have ever been witness to the birth of your child, I think you will agree it's one of the greatest experiences of unconditional love. Your child comes into this world defenseless and totally dependent on you and others. As a parent, you put the needs of your child foremost, and you love your child with no reservations.

After my son was born and as we were preparing to take him home from the hospital, I was changing his diaper. As I lifted his butt up to place a fresh diaper underneath him, he suddenly peed straight up and it hit me in the face. Of course, I couldn't be angry. This defenseless, unknowing, beautiful new being of life had just peed in my face, and I loved him even more. Debbie and I laugh at this example of loving unconditionally.

As our children grow up, they will do great things and they will make mistakes. They will thrill us and disappoint us. We still love them as much as the first day they came into this world. They may frustrate us at times, and confuse us as well, but never once do we love them any less. Being a parent is the best lesson on how to love and be loved unconditionally. There are times when you may not like your child, but you still love him or her.

Many of us understand how adolescence transforms our children. As they grow into their teenage years, they believe they know everything, and we as parents know *nothing*. It's a season most parents endure. My son and I clashed more often than I care to admit. It's not something I'm proud of. I know at times I push him and my daughter really hard to be the best they can be. I can be an overbearing parent, but it's only because I want the best for them. There are days when my children are in no mood for my admonitions or opinions, but I push anyway. Often, I end up saying "I'm sorry," and they are always willing to forgive me. When that happens, I don't feel good about it, but we always say "I love you" before going to bed.

Committing to Unconditional Love

I read a wonderful story about unconditional love on the *Moral Stories* website that I think perfectly illustrates my philosophy on the topic.

The story goes something like this: There was a man who married a beautiful woman years ago. Not long after they were married, she developed a skin disease. At some point during the marriage and as the disease progressed, the husband started pretending to lose his eyesight and eventually to be blind. He did this because he loved her and didn't care about her beauty: He knew that she would suffer more from the fear of how she looked than she would from the disease itself, and he wanted to spare her that worry. She died young, but during their time together, he continued to love her as always. She cared for and loved him as well, all the while thinking he needed her help to get around, but no longer fearing that her loss of beauty would steal his love from her. They enjoyed a happy life as long as they both lived.

Sometimes it is good for us to act blind and ignore one another's shortcomings in order to be happy. Beauty will fade with time, but the heart and soul will always be the same. Love people for what they are from the inside, not from the outside.

When a couple gets married, they say vows to each other: "for better, for worse, for richer, for poorer, in sickness and in health, til death do us part." This is a commitment to unconditional love. No matter what happens, the couple is committing to stay together.

Many believe no one can ever love unconditionally as God has loved us. However, I believe we have a lifelong journey in learning or attempting to love each other that way. Think about how you love others. I might wonder at a specific moment, *Do I love this person unconditionally? Am I judging someone unfairly?* When we are in a state of judgment, we do not love unconditionally. Next time you are frustrated with someone or something, ask yourself those two questions and really reflect on how you love others.

It can also be *freeing* to be able to love without conditions or judgment. When you love unconditionally, you become a person of strength, meaning you are not willing to fall into society's trap of holding a grudge or loving conditionally. Think about being the father in the story of the prodigal son. Consider the fact that one day you may experience something similar with your child. You have taught your child values and lessons all his life, and one day your son gets up and leaves. You let him go because you are aware in your heart that he needs to go through this, and you also know he will return one day once he comes to his senses. And when he does, this brings a sense of fulfillment and joy to you. Loving unconditionally frees us from the grasp of that poison. We all want to live a life of freedom, and if we really work hard at it, we can experience this freedom at a high level. That's ultimately what we all want!

REFLECTION QUESTIONS

- Reflect on your life and think about times when you were loved unconditionally. What did that feel like?
- Were you able then to recognize moments when you could have loved unconditionally?
- Do you have a habit of judging others? If so, what could you do differently to eliminate that habit?

INNER FREEDOM

WHAT IS INNER FREEDOM and what does it feel like? It's a feeling of knowing things are going to be okay no matter what happens in your life. It's a place of calm in your heart, a place of peace and contentment. When you are aware of these moments, and you no longer have moments of anxiety no matter the circumstances in your life, you can experience inner freedom.

What would it be like to live a life of freedom? Freedom to be not only what you *want* to be, but who you are *supposed* to be. Bigger yet is the awareness that this possibility exists. That is one of the toughest goals to which anyone can strive. If you could be free of all the junk that clutters your mind, imagine the life you would live.

Surrender and Discipline

People tend to believe inner freedom is this place of bliss and glee that looks beautiful and easy, and although it can be that, it's a grind to get there. You don't just wake up one morning and say, *I have inner freedom now!* It takes hard work. And it starts with surrendering.

You might think I'm crazy right now, but think about it. In general when people think about the word "surrender," they think about throwing up the proverbial white flag. They think it's giving up or giving in. Most of us think of it as surrendering from something. You have to think counterintuitively. By surrendering, you aren't giving up, you are going with the flow. You are not fighting the current. And when we go with the flow things seems to come with a little more ease. However, it takes discipline to get there.

I think of setting and accomplishing goals. You can't set a goal and haphazardly get there. You have to have discipline to do what's required to get there. The word discipline sounds restrictive and on the surface maybe it is. But when you have discipline and you achieve the goals you set out to achieve, you will feel a sense of freedom. I talked earlier in the book about losing weight and when people would ask me how I did, I would tell them I was on the discipline diet. It takes discipline to be good at something or to achieve something.

When thinking of finances, the word budget comes to mind. People see a budget as restrictive also, but if you have the discipline to stick to a budget (if you restrict yourself now) you will have financial freedom later. It's counterintuitive. People budget their money and their time more than anything else, and they do this to gain a sense of freedom.

So I take you back to surrender. It takes discipline to stay on the road of surrender long enough to find that sense of inner freedom we're all after. And when you're on that road, you don't feel like you have any control, but you do. You live life with an open hand and an open heart. You're not holding on to things tightly and this, again, gives you a sense of freedom.

You can develop the skill of surrendering over time by practicing, and the life you lead right now is already the perfect practicing ground. Things come at us all day long. We have fires to put out and issues to resolve all the while trying to make a living, raise a family, and pay the bills. Surrendering to this reality is a way to create inner freedom in your life. When a situation comes at you, see it for what it is and practice surrendering—in other words, just go with it. As you become more aware in general, you can discipline yourself to be especially aware of the moments that you could surrender to. You might not want to surrender, but after contemplating the situation and the outcomes (surrendering versus fighting it), surrendering is usually the better option. Begin today to learn the art of surrendering and soon you will experience inner freedom at a deeper level.

Now we will continuously veer off course, needing adjustments along the way. When the U.S.A. first sent men to the moon, they were off course much of the time. The astronauts had to continuously recalibrate to stay the course. The same happens for each one of us in our lives. We need to learn to embrace this concept.

I sit here at times and think about all the books I have read and all the years and study of personal growth I've experienced, and I continue to ask myself these questions: *Why am I not further down the road than I am? Why am I not on target to hit my goals?* So, it's all relative, right? What does that statement mean? Further down the road in comparison to what? Well, further down the road than where *I* think I should be.

When I'm having these feelings, I'm actually setting up a roadblock to allowing myself to experience fulfillment and joy in who I am and what I experience. This is where I have to recalibrate my thinking: This is where I tap into my discipline around surrendering to what is. If I can accept where I'm at in the moment and trust that if I continue to do what I'm doing knowing in time things are going to be fine, then I can allow myself to experience the fulfillment I desire.

Surrendering Leads You to Breakthroughs

I have been recently listening to some Wayne Dyer CDs, and something that struck me in one of them was a comment he made about being in a state of flow or a state of allowing. What does that mean? Have you ever prayed or wished for patience? What happens when you do? Well, opportunities and challenges present themselves to you to give you the opportunity to practice patience. Being in a state of flow or allowing is similar. Say for instance something goes wrong in your day. You had something planned, and out of nowhere an unexpected surprise comes your way. Instead of complaining about it, you just go with it. You go with the flow. If you commit yourself to this practice, challenges will present themselves that look negative on the surface, but in reality they are opportunities for you to embrace the flow.

I decided to commit to this state of allowing. I was willing to surrender to this. So, I decided to read the book *Trustful Surrender to Divine Providence* (Father Jean Baptiste Saint-Jure & Blessed Claude De La Colombiere & Paul Garvin [Prof.]) It's about surrendering to His will or allowing, accepting what is, and staying in the flow. Being in the present moment and allowing what is to be. This is an advanced acceptance practice.

I talked earlier about Robbie's breakthrough from reading *Training Camp* and how the story of Martin, the main character in the book, resonated with him. Before Martin could have his breakthrough, he had to face his deepest fear.

In the story one of Martin's coaches from the same book, Coach Ken, wants Martin to share his fears, his deepest fears, and Martin resists until he reads Coach Ken's playbook on life, not football. He discovers his own deepest fear of not being loved and finally shares it with Coach Ken. As I was reading this, I was putting myself in Martin's shoes, thinking about what's held me back from being further along in my life than I think I should be. I realized that I was not experiencing inner freedom because I had not surrendered to the idea that I was loved.

Now I was already reading another book at the time, which I would read in the mornings, and I didn't want to veer off from that so I decided to additionally read a few pages each night of *Training Camp* before retiring to bed. I rose from bed one Saturday morning with plans to get some work done and work out. My typical routine when I get up in the morning is to spend some quiet time in my home office, plan my day, and then do some work. Something was nudging me to read *Training Camp* that Saturday morning. As I walked from the bathroom past my bed to my office, I was being pulled to the nightstand to pick up the book. As much as I wanted to get started with my other priorities of the day, the pull toward reading the book took me down another path.

I picked up the book, walked into my office, and sat in my chair. I read my typical three to five pages, but something continued to nudge me to keep reading. Thirty pages later, I understood the fear Martin had in the story and how it related to me, causing emotion to well up inside me.

As I was reading, I thought about all my years of doing things to please others. I thought about all the things I haven't done in fear of what others might think. I thought about all the books I have read over the years and all the times I've questioned why I wasn't further down the road than I felt I should have been. I had been a people pleaser all my life. I didn't want to disappoint people or let people down! What had held me back from becoming the best version of myself? I was fearful of the same thing. Fearful of not being loved! I was not allowing myself to experience inner freedom because I was locking myself down in fear of not being loved if I didn't do things to please others.

Tears welled up in my eyes; in fact, they came pouring out. As I was reading, I was thinking back to what had happened to me in the last four weeks. I read and heard those words of letting go, being in a state of flow, and surrendering. When I committed to it, things started happening. The first morning I decided to commit, I had a tenant from one of my rental properties call and tell me the heat wasn't working in the house. I had a real estate deal fall apart. I had some issues at work, and I felt like things were going in the opposite direction of what I expected. I was supposed to be in the state of flow and everything was going to go smoothly. NOT! I had told my wife about my commitment and what was happening, and she encouraged me to stay with it even though it was just the first day. At ten o'clock that evening, she asked me if I was okay as we were about to go to bed. I said yes, of course, and then a minute later I received a text from another tenant informing me that the roof was leaking on that house. I could only laugh.

As the next few weeks moved along, a few more real estate deals fell apart and there were more stresses at work. I went running one day and a few hours later I couldn't walk only to find out I had partially torn the labrum in my hip. I had numbness in my leg and foot. I visited a chiropractor. She told me my back was not in alignment. An "ah-ha" moment! I was not in alignment physically, emotionally, and spiritually. But I was getting there, and these were the things I had to go through to get there.

As I continued to reflect that Saturday morning on what had occurred those last few weeks, I decided to get on my hands and knees, and I prayed to have the strength to surrender and let go of all those fears. All the emotion came rushing out. I cried like a child. When we have these fears, all we have to do is let God in our hearts. He is always there waiting for us to let Him in, and we resist because of the fear or pride we have.

After a few moments I thought about what had transpired over the last hour. I wanted to capture everything that had just happened, so I went to my computer and began typing as fast as I could.

As I finished typing, there was a knock at my office door. It was my son, who had just risen from bed. He stuck his head in the door to say good morning. He saw the tears in my eyes and asked if everything was okay. I asked him to sit down so we could talk for a few minutes. We talked about his phone call to me regarding his breakthrough about his skydiving experience and how it related to the book. I then asked him if he remembered the part of the book he'd read prior to his breakthrough.

He said, "Yes, about fear?" I acknowledged that and then began asking him questions.

Years ago, he had come to me to tell me he did not want to live a parent-centered life anymore. He wanted to live a principle-centered life. He wanted to stop living his life to please his mom and me. He wanted to live his life based on his desires.

So I took him back to that evening and asked him, "What were you afraid of most back then?" He said he was fearful of letting us down. I responded by telling him it was deeper than that.

He thought for a few seconds and then responded, "I was afraid of disappointing you and Mom."

I looked him in the eyes and said, "Robbie, I think it's deeper than that. What were you really afraid of?"

He thought for a minute as he had his head down. Then he turned his head, looked at me, and said, "I was afraid you and Mom wouldn't love me."

I looked at him and tears started flowing again. He got up from his chair, walked over to me, and asked me to give him a hug. There we stood, hugging each other as all the emotion flowed from me.

If it were not for him sharing his breakthrough, I would not have read the book again and I would not have had my own breakthrough. And, we would not have had the experience we had that morning. Everything affects everything! I could now see how everything that occurred over that time period was connected, and I was even more convinced of my need to surrender.

When we place our trust in God, good things happen. The trials and challenges we face are our workout in the gym. We have to tear the muscle down before we can build it up to be stronger. We can be a resistor in life or a conductor. When we choose to be the conductor, the energy flows and we can experience this inner freedom. And ultimately, when we know we're loved, we can allow ourselves to experience the fulfillment we desire. Ultimately, we experience freedom to be who we are.

Don't Just Accept It—Embrace It!

Inner freedom is always within reach if we only take the time to understand and embrace the idea of it. But it's not just embracing "it." It's about embracing and accepting who you are—all your good qualities and all your shortcomings. By embracing it, I'm talking about more than just accepting—I'm talking about wrapping your arms around this idea figuratively and really digging into it. Our idiosyncrasies define who we are. When we can look in the mirror and not just accept but truly like what we see, we experience the freedom to be who we are.

Always know we have an inner voice that constantly bombards us with fear and doubt, but at other times can fill us with hope and inspiration. I believe these good ideas are coming from a higher power, and we need faith that things will work out when we listen to that voice of inspiration. The doubting voice, on the other hand, may come from insecurity or a lower self-worth.

For decades, I have been reading and studying personal growth material. I'm a positive person, yet I still have my insecurities. I have built a shell around myself with all this knowledge and experience, but I have also shielded my lower sense of self-worth from others. Once I admitted I struggled with that, I freed myself to be who I am. I continue to work through the process of becoming the best version of myself. The freedom is in the transparency and the acceptance and, most importantly, the awareness of it all. You can never solve a problem if you don't know the cause. You find the cause by becoming aware of it, and that's why awareness is the foundation of this book. We can put Band-Aids on things all day long, but sooner or later the Band-Aid has to come off, exposing the wound.

There is nothing like feeling free to be who you are. There is even more joy in embracing it.

Barriers to Inner Freedom

At times, you are kept from your inner freedom. For instance, you may be distracted with a worry or concern. If you hold on to that distressing thought for any period of time, you are allowing it to control your state of mind. So much of your energy becomes focused on the distraction you cannot function at full capacity. You become a hostage to the thought or worry.

For instance, maybe you must make a tough decision to let someone go from a job. You may have anxiety about how the process of firing someone will transpire. You might be thinking, *What is going to happen to him financially if I fire him? How is this going to affect his family? What is he going to think of me?* These are all common concerns that could hold you back or dominate your thinking. What you are really fearful of is not being liked in the moment you make that decision. These thoughts make you a prisoner of fear and worry. Sure, firing someone is unpleasant, but the goal is to make the organization stronger. It must be done. You may procrastinate for hours or even days to avoid a tough conversation. These worries hold you back from accomplishing *other* tasks awaiting you, and they sap away the energy required to have a successful day. All of this deprives you of your inner freedom.

What is the best way to handle this situation? Tackle it head on! The longer we procrastinate, the more ineffective we become.

I recently changed insurance coverage from a company I had been with for years. Everything was fine with the current company. I loved the people I was working with and their service. But I developed a friendship with a gentleman who owned his own insurance business. For a period of ten years, we had been in the same circles. Once I decided I was going to make the change, I agonized over the thought of taking my business to another company. For a week or so, I vacillated as to how I was going to handle it and what I was going to say. Worrying about this every day was draining and took energy from other priorities needing my attention. I allowed myself to be held captive by the anxious indecision to act.

Each day, from the time I made the decision, I intended to make the change. But I woke up with anxiety about making the call. I didn't *want* to fire the company, or my agent for that matter. She had done nothing wrong. It was a matter of circumstance and worrying about how she would feel about me. Her boss was also a friend of mine who had referred me business in the past, and I worried that I would be damaging that relationship as well. When I awoke in the morning, I resolved to make the call, but I couldn't muster up the courage to do so. I did this *every* morning for a *week* before I finally contacted my agent.

Once I made the call, a weight lifted from my shoulders and I felt this tremendous relief. I had freed myself. I had allowed this anxiety and worry to dominate my thinking for an *entire week*. I was more afraid of not being loved than I was of doing what needed to be done.

What is holding *you* back on a daily basis? Is it a career change? Is it just telling someone you can't do something? Some of us have a huge problem saying "no," and we let our anxiety build, fearing that "no" will make us disliked. If something doesn't line up with our goals or values, the answer should be easy. Yet we torture ourselves into thinking otherwise. When we are in alignment with our values, when we choose the path of surrender, we should feel a sense of peace and confidence in our decisions—free to move on from the moment.

Is Money the Answer?

There are many people who equate money with freedom and fulfillment. You may be thinking, *If only I had this amount of money, I would feel fulfilled.* I would pause for a moment and think about that. In the past, I have spoken to friends who have had a great deal of financial success. During our conversations the subject of fulfillment and freedom was discussed. In two specific instances my friends told me they were financially secure and would never have to worry about money again, yet they were feeling unfulfilled. They both felt they were trapped in their careers with no way out. Yes, they are financially set, but are they experiencing freedom the way they desire? Now their job is to discover what fulfills them and pursue that.

Giving and Receiving Love

Finally, allow yourself to love and be loved. This means to *love unconditionally* and to receive love with open arms. Learning how to give and receive forgiveness plays a huge part in this. When we've been wronged in some way, it can be extremely difficult to forgive the offender. It's even harder to forgive when the offense is gravely serious or drastic. Without forgiving, we can create a poison within us, and it spreads as we continue to feed it with bitterness. The bitterness will consume you and eventually hold you captive to everything you think, do, and feel. You will be a prisoner of your own device.

Once you decide to forgive, releasing the bitterness and expelling the poison, a sense of love will overcome you, allowing you the freedom to move forward.

When I lost the $450,000 I spoke about earlier, I beat myself up for years. It took a long time before I was able to accept it as part of my journey and forgive myself. *How could I have let that happen?* was the question that plagued me. *How could I do that to my family?* It happened, and I learned from it, and now I am a better person because of it. I thought my wife was going to despise me for allowing it to happen, but she forgave me instead and said, "I trust you. I know we will be okay, and I know you will come back from this." Those were powerful words to hear, and to know Debbie trusted in me enough was all I needed to believe it would all work out. In my mind, I thought, *If Debbie could forgive me, why shouldn't I forgive myself?* I wasn't freed of the guilt of losing the money until I was able to accept her forgiveness and chose to forgive myself. Her words and her trust helped me to do that. More than that, was I afraid to tell her about the losses because of the losses or because I was thinking she wouldn't love me anymore?

Freedom is a choice. When something unfortunate happens in our lives and we fail to get past it, we imprison ourselves. We can choose how to respond positively, and when we do, freedom is the gift we receive. This book isn't about any single process to inner freedom; it's about a journey, and the path through a life of experiences. It's about becoming aware of and reflecting on all of life's experiences and how that will lead to a fulfilling life.

There will be peaks and valleys, and sometimes you may feel as if you've gone three steps forward and two steps back. Or you may feel as though you've moved two steps forward and three steps back. In either case, embrace the moment. Allow yourself to experience the growth in each lesson, and this will lead you to a place of peace.

REFLECTION QUESTIONS

- What barriers are holding you back from experiencing inner freedom?
- Going forward, what will you decide to surrender to?
- Are you aware of the moments when you need to recalibrate?
- When in your life have you not gone after your heart's desires in fear of disappointing someone?
- Is there anyone in your life from whom you have withheld your forgiveness? How could your life be better if you did offer that forgiveness?

CHAPTER 16

MAKE THE COMMITMENT

YOU HAVE JUST finished reading through several stories of my life and the lessons I have learned, and hopefully you were able to discover how some of the stories in your life lead to some of your enlightening moments. My hope is you will read this book more than once, and in doing so, you will absorb the lessons behind the stories. You will discover how to connect the dots of some of your very own stories, and you will grow with each experience. There is no formula, just the processes of life you go through. You may have experienced some highs and lows of your own and may be asking yourself, *Now what?*

Make a commitment!

Making a commitment to work on becoming aware of your life's experiences and reflecting on the meaning of those experiences is the surest route to living a fulfilling life. It will not only impact you, it will impact the lives around you. People will be inspired by you to do the same for themselves and then live the best life they can live to impact and improve the lives of others around them.

A Story of Commitment

Back in 2009, Robbie began to show some interest in watching football with me. We would watch a couple games here and there during the season. As the season moved along, Robbie asked me if we could watch the upcoming Super Bowl together. I was elated! So I made a commitment to him that he and I would watch it together. The Super Bowl was scheduled to be played on February 7, 2010.

Months earlier I had scheduled a golf trip with a group of friends in Orlando, Florida, during Super Bowl week, and I was scheduled to return home the evening before the game. Weather reports suggested there would be snow the weekend prior to the Super Bowl and possibly more during the week. Getting to Florida wasn't a problem, but returning on time for the big game was a concern depending on the weather. The first storm of the week happened to be a blizzard, which dumped a significant amount of snow in Baltimore. Now the other storm was brewing, and I couldn't recall ever having two blizzards within such a short period of time, so I was trying not to worry about it.

As the game weekend approached, it was pretty certain we were going to get hit with another big snowstorm. It was Saturday morning, and I was playing my final round of the week. I was going to fly out that evening. As we were playing, I received a text from the airline canceling all flights to Baltimore because of the incoming storm, and yes, it would be another blizzard. Now I had to figure out how I was going to get home in time to watch the Super Bowl with my son and honor my commitment.

I called the airlines to try to fly into other airports closer to Baltimore so that I could fly in and then rent a car to drive the rest of the way home. Nothing was available, and the earliest I could fly home would be Tuesday. I was disappointed that I wouldn't be able to get home, and I felt terrible that I wouldn't be able to watch the game with Robbie. I called home to give Debbie the news. She would have to tell Robbie I was stuck in Florida.

After dinner that evening I made a decision. The only way I was going to get home in time to honor my commitment to my son was to drive from Florida. I asked the guys to take me to the airport, where I would rent a Tahoe and drive straight through the night to get home. I called Debbie to let her know of my plan, and I asked her not to let Robbie know so I could surprise him when I arrived home. I left the airport at 10 p.m. and started my drive to Baltimore.

I was exhausted, but I was determined to get home in time for the game and I knew I would encounter tougher driving conditions as I got closer to home. I called Debbie to let her know when I was almost home and I was going to knock on the door when I got there. My plan was to have her let Robbie answer the door when I knocked, as I was excited to see the look on his face when he opened the door. At 3:30 p.m., just three hours before the Super Bowl was to start, I knocked on the door. When Robbie opened the door, he had the biggest look of surprise on his face and gave me a huge hug. We were going to watch our first Super Bowl together!

This story is about a commitment I made to my son to watch a football game. The point is that it was a commitment I made and one that I honored. What could happen if you made commitments in all areas of your life and honored them? It would have a huge impact on you and those around you. Now, I'm asking you to make a commitment to yourself to reflect on your life and be aware of all the good you have experienced. Take the time to reflect and journal your thoughts and experiences. I want you to give yourself the gift of awareness and see how that can lead you to experience a more fulfilling life.

I want you to be able to look back on your life stories and experiences and feel the joy and the fulfillment of what occurred. It will be in the awareness of all that you experienced that, when you reflect on what happened, good or bad, the lessons you have learned, and the people who have been there for you along the way, you will realize that God is the maestro of your life and that your life is, and always has been, better than you think. Then you will experience that fulfillment you've been searching for.

Understand that life happens—you will experience the peaks and valleys in life, and you may not always feel fulfilled. But the idea is to become aware of what is happening and why. If you haven't already, I encourage you to download the free companion workbook at robcommodariauthor.com/workbook so you have a starting place for your reflections. Hopefully you'll enjoy the practice so much you'll continue with journaling more extensively.

Whether you are young or maybe middle-aged, or even in the latter part of your life, there is still time to reflect on your life and the experiences you have had and become aware of all the great things that have occurred and the lessons you can learn. Your life has been rich and will continue to be rich with experiences. Don't waste another minute to discover all the goodness that surrounds you! Now go live the fulfilling life you are supposed to live and see that your life is better than you think. God bless!

AUTHOR NOTE

Dear Reader:

Thank you so much for spending your time with me. I hope you enjoyed reading *Better Than You Think*. I wrote this book because I wanted to share with you how important awareness is in our lives. If we take the time to reflect on the experiences of our lives and the lessons inside each experience, we will see our lives are better than we think.

When I looked back at all the experiences and stories in my life, it helped me see how good things really are. There have been tough times and now I have nothing but gratitude for those times. There were stories of awesome experiences and there were lessons to learn from that as well. Traveling down this journey of personal growth has led to many breakthroughs for me and by sharing my stories I hope you can resonate with them and truly see how good your life is, too.

The ability to increase your awareness ends only when you have breathed your last breath. I ask you to make a commitment to become more aware of who you are, what makes you tick, and what your hearts desires are. And when you do, you will certainly be on the path of living a more fulfilling life.

It would mean a great deal to me if you would take just a few minutes to rank this book and post your honest review on Goodreads.com and/or the retail site where you purchased the book, like Amazon.com. Reviews are critical for us authors— not only do they help other readers decide if the book might be right for them, your feedback shows us how well we are connecting with our readers. And connecting with readers is what writing is all about!

In thanks for your support, I'd love to gift you with a free copy of the companion workbook for *Better Than You Think*. Just go to www.robcommodariauthor.com/workbook and it's yours. Signing up to receive the companion workbook will also add you to my mailing list so that we can stay in touch about future books, appearances, and more. I look forward to getting to know each other.

Sincerely,

Rob Commodari

ACKNOWLEDGEMENTS

IF IT WERE NOT for the encouragement, the accountability, my journey in personal growth, and the people I've met along the way, I may not have persevered to finish this book.

A special thanks to the following people:

To my wife Debbie and my children, Crystal, Robbie, and Amanda, who have blessed me with so much love and so many of the stories I've shared in this book. I have been blessed with the experiences and the awareness of the lessons they have taught me in life. They are my inspiration.

To Tom & Elizabeth Monteleone whom if I hadn't met, this book might still be just an idea.

To Joe and Paula Erhmann, who encouraged me to write and share my story.

To Curtis Oakes, who taught me to listen to that voice inside.

To Valentino Fernandez, who doesn't know the impact he has had on me. Val introduced me to my first personal growth book, which changed the course of my life.

To Fr. Larry Gesy, who was the priest I spoke to when I returned from college a lost and confused person. Fr. Gesy introduced me to the idea of setting goals and writing affirmations.

To my Mastermind group of Mark Pallack, Mark Brodinsky, and Pete Kohlasch, who for the last six years have encouraged me to complete this book.

To Kelli Snyder of Buffini and Company, who has coached me for almost ten years and is a constant source of encouragement.

To Brian Buffini for the inspiration and encouragement he has provided throughout the years to share my story.

To Sharon Kehnemui for all the time and guidance she gave me in helping me with this book.

To Ally Machate and the entire Writer's Ally team for their patience and guidance in the writing and editing of this book.

To Emily Hitchcock and the Storehouse Media team for their guidance and encouragement on designing the interior and exterior of this book.

To Vicki Adang of The Writer's Ally and her encouragement for me to keep pushing forward to become a better writer.

ABOUT THE AUTHOR

Confused about what to do in life after graduating from college in 1990, Rob discovered a passion for reading. He has since read over 800 books on personal growth and development. Rob's mission in life is to help people discover their unique gifts and abilities in life and to help people use those gifts to reach their fullest potential. Awareness is the key. It was by developing his own awareness that led Rob through his successful careers in the newspaper business, a cigar business and ultimately into his real estate business. Rob Commodari is currently the owner of The Commodari Group real estate team in Maryland. He has been in the business for over 18 years helping people buy and sell residential real estate. He is married to his beautiful wife, Debbie and is the father of three. Rob lives in Perry Hall, Md. Be sure to log in to Rob's website for free gifts and updates on his speaking engagements at www.robcommodariauthor.com.